I SHOULD'VE LEFT WHEN...

Take a journey through my intimate, real-life dating experiences, on a path to positive and productive partnerships.

Yolanda,
thank you so much
for supporting! I hope
you enjoy! *Lov',*
Mimi

Mimi Mansfield

Please contact www.shouldveleft.com.

Library of Congress Cataloging-In-Publication Data

Mansfield, Mimi

I Should've Left When.../Mimi Mansfield

ISBN 978-1-5136-4236-9

1. Biographies & Memoirs   2. Romance & Erotica

Library of Congress Control Number: 2019909176

Cover and interior design: Stacey Grainger

Printed in the United States of America

First Edition

CONTENTS

DEDICATION

I'd like to dedicate this novel to my tremendously perfect parents – love you dearly. As you celebrate over 45 years of marriage, you are a true example of love and dedication to family. A sincere thank you.

I also dedicate this novel to my fierce network of ladies!! What a significant support system you are! Thank you for always being there for me and for your continued interest in my dating stories over the years. Your love of my dating stories inspired me to complete this book – a goal I never imagined I could achieve. I hope the relationship stresses we have endured will help us grow. I also hope that happily ever after lies ahead for us all – even if that means together in a Golden Girl's house!

AUTHOR'S FOREWORD

For some ladies, long-lasting love comes easy... They meet their Mr. Right in the process of completing their schooling, and in their early 20s, they're off to wedded bliss. Ahhh... They manage to find one of the good ones: a faithful, doting, man who is easy on the eyes – heck, maybe he's even financially secure. He's the "once in a lifetime" guy who brings you a healthy, happy relationship "'til death." And then, ladies... there's the rest of us. Our experience finding Mr. Right is a long, windy, seemingly endless road. One filled with potholes, speed bumps, detours and a bunch of crazy-bad drivers.

Whether married or single, most of us can relate to one thing: experiencing some "not so great" times in our personal relationships. And many of us can remember a breaking point in that prior relationship, feeling like "I should leave this ـــــــ [wonderful soul?]," but we stay, oftentimes longer than we should.

I happen to be one of those girls who has had more than a few lemons in my dating life. And I am absolutely one of those girls who can admit to staying longer than I should have. For example, **I should've left when** I saw he had a 520 credit score and no desire to improve it, or when his apartment was so atrocious that I didn't want to sit down, or definitely when I found another woman's (ugly) shoes in his bedroom – obvious. Although I stayed with each of these men too long, I can say that every man I dated has had a purpose in my life. I ultimately found a way to turn those lemons into lemon drop martinis. "Bad credit score guy" was my key to meeting some of the BEST friends in my life today. "Atrocious apartment guy"– well, there, I learned to take a break after a break-up and not jump to the next "atrocious" guy, and "Women's shoes in the bedroom guy" (aka "Radio Shack") taught me to follow my instincts and that the truth – or the ugly shoes – will always come out in the end.

No one has a magic solution to finding a good partner, nor can anyone tell you whether you should stay in a relationship. I initially set out to write this book purely for entertainment purposes – to laugh at the stupid things I've done in relationships. But through the writing process, I've realized that someone might benefit from reading my crazy dating stories. Whether you're looking for some-one new or you're assessing your current state, I hope this book helps you navigate the relationship waters a little better. Perhaps you will notice a pattern in your partner-selection process that you want to change (I know I did). Taking a break from dating for at least a year can help you press the reset button and potentially end an unproductive trend. And if you're happily hitched, I hope you will still find a few takeaways from this book, even if it simply helps you hold on to your husband/significant other that much tighter because you know you have found a gem!

This first installment of MiMi's Dating Adventures finds me at age 38, happily single, but never turning down the opportunity to con-nect with someone new. I start the book in January with a man I've dubbed "Vegas" and end it in December with "57." (You'll un-derstand the names as you read along.) While there are four main "characters" in this book, there are parallel storylines and several guys within each section.

Throughout the book, I identify the good things about each guy, the crazy things I did, and the red flags that made my intuition alarm blare out, "Abort, abort!" like a Titanic evacuation siren. All the flags and signs I log about the guys and myself are summarized at the front of the book, so feel free to flip to the front as you read! Future installments of Mimi's Dating Adventures will travel back in time to my 20s and early 30s, featuring "Credit Score," "Radio Shack," and a whole host of other characters, so stay tuned!

As you read this book, I want you to laugh, I want you to gasp, and ultimately, I hope you can relate in some way to the journey that many of us women go through on the path to choosing positive partners.

Now it's time to grab a glass of wine (or that lemon drop martini) and dive into my intimate real-life dating experiences!

Note: Character names and situations have been changed to protect the guilty.

Love,

A Collection of Relationship Turn-ons, Turn-offs,
"Owning My Crazy" and My Intuition Alarms

Dating Turn-on List

A man who...

1. Shows interest up-front – makes the first move, gives good eye-contact, gives gentle physical touches in appropriate areas (back, arms, etc.), offers compliments, locks in the subsequent touchpoint or date.

2. Looks out for you upon meeting you – offers a drink, walks you to your car, makes sure you get home okay.

3. Knows the limits upon first meeting you – doesn't try to kiss you, get in your car, or worse, invite you over for "a nightcap." He takes things slowly.

4. Shares important fundamentals in common with you (e.g., views on having children, politics, religion, etc.) Also, he shares communication patterns with you. #qualitytime

5. Can plan! Cheers to the man who can plan – make a dinner reservation, book a flight, plan a picnic, anything!

6. Is outraged by another man's poor behavior. Condemns cheating friends or, even better, does not keep them in his circle.

7. Is thoughtful. Even small "just because" gifts can go a long way. Especially if gifts are your love language.

8. Enjoys the same types of activities as you (e.g., adventures, sports, social activities, outdoor activities, cultural activities, listening to the same kind of music, dancing, photography, etc.)

9. Is transparent. Shares important details of his personal life early on (wife/exes, kids, who he lives with, etc.). Keeps surprises to a minimum.

10. Has the same dietary habits as you. Don't get me wrong – I love fried chicken on occasion, but I'm not trying to support your unhealthy eating habits on the regular.

11. Takes the lead! I love a man who can take charge (e.g., carrying a conversation in a social setting) and make me feel like a lady.

Dating Turn-off/ Red Flag List

1. Consistent spelling, grammatical, or pronunciation errors. Sorry, not sorry.

2. "Let's get a room" guy. Yeah, let's not. Just met you.

3. Quick mood changes – he can go 0-60 in seconds. Can be good... or can be bad.

4. Fundamental differences on major topics (e.g., children, politics, religion, even pets). Or different tastes in things that are important to you (e.g., dietary choices, drinking, smoking, taste in music, etc.)

5. He sued his ex over money, but his lawsuit doesn't seem justified. Men complain about women taking all of their

assets in a divorce; high-earning women have the same issue of men taking them to the bank. I prefer a man who doesn't try to take more from the relationship than he brought into it. To the extent you can carve it out, take what you brought into it and keep it moving.

6. Obsessive compulsive disorder (OCD) tendencies. A lot of us have some level of OCD – I like items in my cabinets and closets relatively organized. But some people have severe cases which can raise the caution flag. I'll blame *Sleeping with the Enemy*.

7. Shows signs of moving too quickly in prior relationships (e.g., got married after being with someone for only a few months). You feel he's on the same fast track with you.

8. Broken promises. Don't commit to a date or tell me you're going to call me and then not follow through. Be a man of your word. If you need to change plans, let me know within a reasonable period of time.

9. I CANNOT do the poor-communication guy. If I call or text you, I need a response within a reasonable period of time. And if your voicemail is constantly full, you're clearly too busy for me.

10. Wants to get kinky too soon. No, I'm not sending you racy photos, nor can we have phone/video or text sex.

11. Sarcasm that borders on disrespect. Or just blatant disrespectful language.

Owning My Crazy

1. Not believing basic facts he says, like, "I'm flying to Dubai." I'm always suspicious. It is undoubtedly due to my insecurities from past relationship trauma.

2. Getting in cars with guys or other alone time too soon after meeting. Guilty, guilty, GUILTY! Being from Philly, I should know better. Basic street smarts.

3. Probably not a good idea to pick up a new guy while out on a date with another guy. My FOMO (Fear of Missing Out) is strong!

4. "Say my name, say my name." I will call you to validate you really are single. I have serious trust issues from prior situations. If you don't pick up the phone late at night, I've got a raised eyebrow, especially if you just texted me.

5. My inability to say no is serious. I can blame Mother Nature, Tito's, or especially Patron for my libido. I can also blame my insane need to please others and not reject his desires. No matter the reason, way too many times I have broken Steve Harvey's 90-day rule for sex – and almost every time, I regret it by the next morning or soon after. I must be better about waiting and not even putting myself in a situation where intimacy could occur until I *really* know a guy.

6. It is so hard for me to break up with a guy. My intuition alarms will be ringing like a five-alarm fire, but I explain my inner thoughts away. My difficulty with hurting others' feelings makes me stay longer than I should – all the time. And then, once I get used to having someone around, it's hard to be alone right after. I have to re-adjust.

7. Doesn't matter how well you think you know a person, do your research! Check all social media for months prior and do a check of local criminal records.

8. I admit that I often play with fire. Once I have ruled a guy as unworthy, I have trouble ending all contact with him. I give too many second chances, thinking they will do better – and they don't.

9. My friends hate that I do this, but I am the queen of the pass-off. If a guy doesn't work for me, but he still has some redeemable qualities, I will refer him to someone new, no problem.

10. I hate to admit it, but I like the thrill of attracting men. I might walk a certain way, dance a certain way, or use my eyes, but I'm a flirt, and I like attention.

11. I cannot stop a moving relationship train. I pretty much jump right on board. I can feel when things are moving too quickly, but it's so hard to stop.

Intuition Alarms

1. "I can't find my driver's license." I felt he was lying to me, and he was.

2. "I've only known you a couple months, but I want to relocate for you. Let's look at houses." I felt it was too soon and that normally, a good man would not move this quickly.

3. The female "friend" who he doesn't tell you about until you find out about her on your own. I felt she was more than a

friend because he didn't mention her naturally in conversation.

4. Little white lies can be indicative of a bigger pattern. When you have that sinking feeling that you're being lied to because stories just don't add up, trust your gut. Run.

5. When you can't get a straight answer and he continues to push you off, changing the topic, or worse, shifting the blame back onto you, he's lying.

6. "Too much, too soon" guy. Shows signs of being highly emotional and falling in love very quickly. You want to believe his strong feelings, and the fact that he wants to spend a lot of time with you is endearing, but it gives you pause.

7. Pay attention to the way a guy treats/treated his ex and his kid(s). If he didn't take care of them (e.g., cheated on his wife, abandoned his child), he won't take care of you.

8. "The eyes have it," as the famous quote goes. Follow your intuition when you look at him face-to-face or even in a photo. When you concentrate, you can sometimes see a sinister stare, which can indicate trouble to come.

9. Over-promises and under-delivers. Offers for expensive vacations, to help with charity, etc., but he never comes through. You can feel his offers are excessive and unrealistic, and you feel they will never pan out.

10. When instinct tells you he's not being honest about something (e.g., if he doesn't answer the phone after he just texted you, if the timelines for his stories don't line up, if he has a certain shady look in his eye, if he hides basic information from you, etc.), follow your feelings. Keep probing until you get answers.

Red-flags for all women:

1. He stops sleeping with you or he sleeps with you much less often/turns down your advances.

2. He starts spending a lot of time with a female acquaintance who he says is "just a friend," but he does not bring her around you.

3. Your parents/family never liked him.

4. He has no true friends of his own.

5. He does not allow you to have girlfriend time.

6. He is not a law-abiding citizen – he has more than moving violations on his record. He has been involved in shady business deals gone bad or serious felonies.

7. You can't take him to a company function for fear he may say or do the wrong thing.

8. He goes out of town "on business" for your birthday, Valentine's Day, or another important time... and he is difficult to reach.

9. He is not available when you need him.

10. He subtly hits on/flirts with other women.

For dating women:

1. Always comes to your house and doesn't invite you to his.

2. He is over 30 and permanently lives with his parents (and it is not for caretaking reasons).

3. He cheated on his last wife/serious girlfriend(s).

4. Everything is perfect – "Mr. Too Good to be True."

5. He paints far-fetched dreams: "Babyface will sing at our wedding; we can fly our wedding party to Fiji."

6. He invites you to his place for the first or second date.

7. He tells you he loves you within the first week of getting to know you.

8. He texts you instead of calling you to set up your first date.

9. He stands you up... multiple times.

10. He asks you to "go Dutch" or pay for him on the first date.

11. You never talk to him after 8:00 p.m., and he always has an excuse: "I was asleep," "I didn't hear my phone."

12. He is over 40 and has never been married... Commitment issues!

13. He asks you for thousands of dollars.

Just not so cute:

1. Bad breath (if you have ever held your breath during sex... Ugh!)

2. Body odor (ever date a guy who smells like mothballs?? Horrific!)

3. Doesn't clean the toilet seat or properly flush after each use... Yuck!

4. His place is deplorable. You don't want to lay your head on his sheets.

5. He has a dead tooth.

CONTINUE THE CONVERSATION BY ADDING YOUR FAVORITES TO MY SITE!

Connect with Mimi at:

Shouldveleft.com

Book of Vegas

Vegas

MANGO'S

It's girls' night out at Orlando's newest nightclub: Mango's Tropical Café – woot woot! And while I love to go out, it's a rainy and cool January night, so I have to force myself to get dressed (though I'm somewhat motivated to wear my new leopard-print dress ☻) and make the 30-minute drive to the hot new nightclub for the first time.

Mango's is packed with people watching the unique, Latin-themed shows downstairs and is filled with people wall-to-wall upstairs, where the Reggaetón and hip-hop dance room is blasting music so loud you can barely talk to the person next to you. Twelve of us ladies, all in our 30s and 40s, are here to celebrate our friend Tana's birthday.

In the upstairs dance room, the infamous red rope separates our group from the large crowd. *Thank you, Tana, for the VIP section – we're too grown-up to be getting stepped on.* While being separated has its privileges, I realize I have a smaller chance of meeting anyone new, which I love to do. Still, as I look around the large crowd for some eye candy, I can't help but notice a tall, suited gentleman staring in my direction. I take a sip of my wine and look away. *Maybe he's looking at someone behind me?* I slowly let my eyes drift back in his direction. Ok, now not only is he looking at me, but he's whispering in his friend's ear, and I get the feeling it's about me. *Hmmm, well I am surrounded by gorgeous women, so maybe he's looking at someone else?* But, then again, I'm used to being singled out. For some reason, guys don't go for the hottest girl in the group; they go for the easiest target, and for some reason, that easy target is often me.

People say it's because I have an inviting smile, but I think I somehow must look like a sucker – a magnet for the liars, cheaters, and jerks of the world, because that is always what I've attracted, like, literally always. From my first boyfriend, who was controlling, and ultimately put his hands on me as he tried to drag me into his parents' basement while telling me that "no one will hear if you scream," to my most recent date, who was in his 50s and who told me during our first and only outing that he had been locked up for child support non-payment years prior, and then he proceeded to NOT pick-up the tab for my burger, I have lived dating nightmares over and over again.

But maybe this time, the outcome will be different. Maybe this guy eyeing me from across the room at Mango's will be a good one – he certainly looks like it.

my crazy #10

I decide to make it easier for the suited gentleman to come and talk to me (if that's what he wants). I move from the far edge of Tana's roped section to the middle and fill up my glass from our shared wine bottle. I then inconspicuously (or so I hope) continue to move over to the opposite edge of the roped area, closer to him, without looking at him. I figure I'm meeting him halfway, but I'm not doing all the work – I don't go to men. And if I'm wrong and he's looking at someone else, I won't look like a fool going up to him. I keep my eye on the dancefloor, watching our friend Nia salsa dance with a much older Dos-Equis-looking guy who is definitely in his glory with her. It's pretty entertaining, so I'm laughing with the girls when I hear in my ear, "You'll have to get out there yourself and dance tonight."

turn on #1

I turn to see my across-the-room-admirer now standing next to me. I smile flirtatiously and respond, "So I guess that means you'll be saving a dance for me then?"

It's an hour later, and we haven't stopped talking – or yelling, I should say, since we are talking over the Reggaetón, which is almost like nails on a chalkboard at this point. I feel guilty for not hanging out with my girlfriends and instead talking to this new guy, but it seems that he and I have so much in common. I don't want to break away. Plus, he is only in town for the night, so I want to learn as much about him as possible.

Vital Statistics:

- ✓ Andrew Henlon, 39
- ✓ Never married, no kids – just like me
- ✓ 6'4" and huge – played college football at Oklahoma State
- ✓ Lives in Las Vegas, where he owns a few homes but grew up in Oklahoma and Texas
- ✓ Works for a beverage company that supplies alcohol to nightclubs, which is why he is at Mango's (I like that reason versus him being a frequent club attendee at our age)
- ✓ He's in Orlando because his company is based here and because he's flying to Dubai the next day (Orlando has a direct flight to Dubai)
- ✓ His family owns a photography business in which he is invested

Check, check, CHECK, I think to myself.

"Do you want to save your number in my phone?" Andrew asks, passing me his iPhone.

"Of course," I respond, with a smile. As I enter my number, I ask him, "So, you're heading to Dubai tomorrow... Have you been before?"

"I have not. This will be my first time."

"Oh, nice. You're going to love it. Dubai is my favorite destination so far." I tell Andrew about my Dubai trip from a few years ago – Sex-and-the-City-style with three girlfriends, as a treat to myself for not failing out of grad school.

"Oh, so then you're an expert. You'll have to tell me where to go while I'm out there," Andrew says with a smile.

We decide to walk around the club since it's my first time here. He seems to have the inside scoop because of his business relationship with the club. "You know," Andrew says, "Pitbull is one of the promoters for the club. He'll be here in April."

"Wow!" I respond. I had just watched Pitbull's New Year's Eve special the week prior. I think he's so cool.

Andrew infers that with his club connections, not only could I come back for the exclusive April concert, but I could also meet Pitbull. Talk about a bonus!

turn on #1

80s music plays in the main club area as Andrew and I continue our walk around Mango's. Maybe it's just me, but I love how Andrew places his hand on the small of my back as we walk through the crowd – it just makes me feel like a lady ☺.

We walk over to the railing, and looking down on the crazy Michael Jackson impersonator show, we continue our conversation. "So, what do you like to do in your spare time, Mimi?" Andrew asks.

turn on #8

"Well, I love to travel, and I love beaches."

Andrew's eyes light up. "Oh? Actually... just a few weeks ago, for Christmas break, I flew to Laguna Beach. I had been working so much, I just needed some downtime, alone," he says.

Interesting. he spent Christmas alone. It sounds a bit sad, and I question (to myself) why he didn't spend it with his family or why he doesn't have anyone special in his life (he is a pretty decent-looking guy after all). But we just met, so I simply respond, "Oh, I used to love Laguna Beach. I spent New Year's there once, back in my 20s." I also loved the MTV show Laguna Beach, but there's no need to mention that ☻. I'm happy to know that Andrew loves the beach, and I put all other questions about his Christmas beach party of one out of my head.

"I should probably get back to my friends. I'm sure they're wondering where I am," I say to Andrew as I finish the mojito he had bought me earlier.

"Sure, let's get you back over there," he says. As we walk back into the dance room, I hear hip-hop music playing. That strong mojito is doing the trick and I can't help but want to dance. I yell over the music to Andrew, "So, someone owes me a dance!"

"That *is* true," he laughs. "Lead the way!"

As we dance, I consciously guide us closer to my friends. I give the girls a wink, letting them know I'm okay. Andrew and I aren't really dancing as much as we're facing each other while swaying back and forth, him with his arms around my waist, and me with one arm loosely around his neck, breaking my neck to look up at him, even in my four-inch heels.

"So, where was your last business trip?" I ask, still trying to learn more about my new acquaintance.

"Well, tomorrow will be my first international business trip; the company has just started a new project there. I typically come here to Orlando four times a year, but my last trip was to Atlanta. I love the Ritz in Buckhead," he says, still dancing with me but looking out into the dancing crowd.

Nice taste, I think to myself. It seems he's bragging a bit, dropping names of high-end places, but at the same time, I appreciate a man who likes the finer things in life. "Nice, I think we have similar tastes," I respond.

I look over to check on my friends, who are starting to close their tabs. "Well, it looks like the evening is winding down," I say, glancing up at my dance partner.

turn on #2

"It is," Andrew responds, "and I need to get some rest for my long flight tomorrow. Can I walk you to your car?"

Ah, he's speaking my language. I love when a guy looks out for me 😊.

"Absolutely. Let me say goodbye to my friends," I respond, feeling guilty for abandoning them for the whole night. I walk over to Tana. "Girl, I'm so sorry!" I explain to her and a couple other girlfriends, hoping they will understand.

"Oh, we're so excited for you. Don't worry about us. I'm glad you had a good time!" my friend Callie responds. I've known this group of ladies for only a couple years, and since most of them are married, they're happy to see me meeting someone who looks like a nice guy. I wanted them to meet Andrew, but we were never close enough to the group for me to introduce him casually, so I let it go.

Walking down the stairs to leave Mango's – Andrew with his hand on the small of my back again – I feel like I've just met one of the nicest men. He has a ride back to his hotel with his co-workers, who were around us the whole night, though I did not meet them. (It was a co-worker he had been whispering to about me when I first felt him staring at me.) After Andrew and I started talking, I noticed him nod to his co-workers a couple times, and they would smile back, showing their approval that he was spending time with me instead of working.

"Oh, here it is," I say as I pull out my pre-paid valet ticket from my purse and hand it to the attendant. Andrew stands by me while my car is being brought up. "So, where are you staying?" I ask.

my crazy #2

"The Marriott by the airport," Andrew responds.

"Wow, that's only five minutes from me," I respond. Now this is where I could get in trouble. Old Mimi might've offered him a ride – I hate to admit it, but I've done it before.

One night, at Universal City Walk, I met a guy who was in town for a conference. We talked briefly and decided to have an impromptu dinner at City Walk to continue the conversation. Afterward, it was late, and years before Uber, so I offered him a ride back to his hotel, partly because of the alcohol, partly because of my nurturing personality, and partly because I can be just plain stupid sometimes. I promised myself I would never put my life at risk like that again by transporting a perfect stranger (who ultimately turned out to be a maniacal liar).

So, standing there with Andrew at Mango's valet, hearing that he is staying at a hotel by my house, I keep my mouth shut. A good man wouldn't ask for a ride anyway – he had come to the club with his co-workers, and he could go back with them no matter how good of a night we had.

"You know, Mimi, my flight isn't until 1:00 tomorrow afternoon. Maybe we could have breakfast in the morning?" Andrew asks.

turn on #1

Love it. He doesn't ask to continue the already late night, but he makes plans to reconnect with me at a decent hour tomorrow. "That would be great!"

On my way home, Andrew texts me, 'Can you let me know your home safe?' Well, he just checked another important box. You won't get a

turn off #1

second date with me unless you make sure I get home ok after the first one 😊. And I try to look past him misspelling 'your,' although that is a pet peeve of mine. I text Andrew once I arrive home so we can finalize our plans to meet for breakfast in the morning. We agree to meet in the lobby of his hotel at 9:00 a.m. But then he continues to text me at 1:30 in the morning.

Andrew: It was really nice meeting you

Me: Very nice mtg you as well. I'm looking fwd to the morning…

Andrew: Likewise. You should be sleepy by now.

Me: Lol been talking to my mom about the evening… about to get ready for bed now 😊

Andrew: You should tell her Vegas says Hi

Me: Haaaa! Omg, how did you know that I use city names for men? And how did you know I told my mom about you?

Andrew: We are fam. Lol

Me: You already know. Nothing like mtg someone you feel comfortable with… regardless of what happens from here…

Andrew: Right. I hate that I have to leave tomorrow. Seems that it was well worth getting to know you.

Me: I know, but hopefully we'll have plenty more time… The beauty of being flexible and free.

[What I meant by this is that neither of us have a significant other or kids – I didn't explain this to him, as I figured he knew what I meant.]

Andrew: Yup. Don't forget to plan your trip to Vegas

Me: August… Your 40ᵗʰ birthday… done.

When Andrew had told me earlier in the evening that he is 39, I asked him when is his 40th, and he said he's going to do a big Vegas birthday party in August. I'm all-in – I love to travel and love to have things to look forward to ☺.

This is my M.O., though: I meet a guy and things escalate rapidly. It sometimes happens with girlfriends, too. I like to think it's because I have an inviting and open spirit that makes people feel comfortable. But what I have found is that all too often, the relationships that start off as "too much, too soon" crash and burn in the fieriest way. I'm hoping that maybe this time with Andrew will be different.

OMELETS

I'm exhausted yet excited (and a little nervous) about seeing Andrew again for breakfast. I really enjoyed talking to him last night at Mango's and am hopeful that things between us are just as good in the light of day. I find the perfect casual khaki-colored dress in my closet to wear – cute but not too much – we're just going to an airport hotel after all. I head out the door for the five-minute drive to his hotel.

I take a seat in the Marriott lobby, watching guests walk by as I wait for Andrew to come down from his room. I'm looking down at my phone, reading work messages, when I feel a presence coming towards me. I look up, and it's Andrew. I find it interesting that I felt him approaching – I feel like it's a sign of positive energy. I'm in a wedge-heel that is much lower than the heels I wore the previous night, and with him being 6'4" and probably close to 300 pounds, it feels like I'm being approached by a giant. I stand up to hug him, and he flashes his warm smile, making him appear like a sweet, cuddly teddy bear. He is "long-flight ready," dressed in a navy collared fleece pullover and sweatpants, with the fleece material adding to his cuddly-bear appeal.

We walk into the Marriott's restaurant and approach the hostess stand. "Party of two?" she asks.

"Yes," Andrew responds. The hostess escorts us to a table toward the back, next to a window and away from most of the other guests. *Perfect*, I think to myself. *We can talk, and people won't know that we're on our first date* ☺. The sun can't be any brighter as it shines through the window at our table. So far, I'm satisfied that I came to meet my new friend of 12 hours for breakfast.

Andrew and I decide to head over to the fresh omelet station, where we order pretty much the same thing – an egg white omelet with cheese and veggies. I'm surprised he's eating so healthy since he is a pretty big guy, but I presume he's trying to watch his diet.

"So, what sites do I need to see while I'm in Dubai this week?" Andrew asks while we're watching our omelets being prepared.

"Oh, well you have to go to the top of the Burj Khalifa and do a desert safari. Oh, and if you can go indoor skiing and hit some good nightclubs, I bet you would enjoy it."

Back at the table, I flip through some of my Dubai photos on Facebook (he doesn't have an fb account), and we continue our conversation. "So, tell me about your family," I request. Turns out Andrew's parents are still married and have been for over 40 years, like my parents, and he has an older brother, like me. *Well, that's pretty cool.*

Taking a bite of his omelet, Andrew asks, "How could it be that you're single? I just don't get it."

I'm used to this question. I'm a decent-looking girl: 5'3", 150 pounds, a perfect size 10, with a good career as a corporate executive. I don't want to tell him that I have a habit of attracting liars, cheaters and thieves, so I simply respond, "Well, I think it has a lot to do with the fact that I don't want children." I might as well get this conversation out of the way. He doesn't have children, and I'm afraid it may be an issue for him. I continue, "While I love children, and I enjoy working with them in my spare time, I've never had a desire to have any of my own. I know it sounds strange. All my friends think I'll change my mind, but that's who I am today, and I don't foresee my feelings changing."

turn on #4

Andrew takes a sip of his orange juice and responds, "Well, not having children shouldn't be a deal-breaker."

"Wow, that's good to know," I say as I breathe a sigh of relief.

turn on #8

Upon leaving the restaurant, I ask Andrew if he's comfortable taking a photo with me. I take pictures constantly, so this is something of a test; if he isn't up for a photo, I know that could be a challenge. Not only does Andrew jump at the opportunity, but he also flags down his co-worker to take our photo. *Perfect.*

After five photo takes in front of his hotel, Andrew reaches out to hug me goodbye. Stepping back from the hug, Andrew asks, "Well, I fly back here to Orlando Friday afternoon. Maybe we can have dinner that night?"

turn on #1

Awesome, I love a guy who can keep me engaged – no dead-space. "I would love that," I respond gleefully.

So, Andrew is piquing my interest in so many ways:

- ✓ He's age appropriate, has no kids and has never been married.

- ✓ He could satisfy my desire for adventure – he's offered a Pitbull concert with a potential meet-and-greet. Plus, I love to take trips, so I'm excited to return to Vegas, as well as to eventually go on other trips with him.

- ✓ Twice, he's locked in subsequent dates with me before we parted ways.

✓ He is incredibly responsive. He's great with regular text and phone calls so far (this is key for me).

✓ He seems to have a calm and gentle personality, as I noticed in his interaction with the waitress and his co-workers.

✓ And, he enjoys taking photos ☺.

my crazy #11

I know I have a habit of falling for guys too quickly. I try to stop myself, but certain men can pull me in by speaking my primary love language: quality time. Andrew is proving to be masterful at giving me quality time. He even texts me from the sky on his way to Dubai.

Andrew: What type of attributes do you look for in a guy?

Me: The main attributes you hit last night:

1. You were not overly assertive in your approach – you used gentle eye contact – you didn't motion for me, you allowed it to happen naturally. Also, I appreciate that you didn't ask me to come to the hotel with you ... you'd be surprised how aggressive and inappropriate some guys are.

2. You were extremely gentlemanly (offering me a drink, guiding me with your hand on my back, walking me to my car, making sure I got home ok).

3. You're very responsive via text ... that is important to me.

4. You enjoy dancing/socializing ... I know there's more but how's that for starters?

Andrew: I'm smiling. You seem really nice and confident. Pretty smile and smart which is really attractive.

Me: Yay, you should be smiling. I'm glad I shared that with you, you deserve to know how amazing you are (or seem to be after 18 hours lol). And yes, my confidence has improved over the years, that's for sure. Would be even better if I lost 10 lbs 😜

Andrew: No, you look great.

Me: So, your list?

Andrew: Honesty, even when it hurts. Loyalty. Genuineness. Smart. Strong personality. Confident. Natural Communication, which all seem to be part of your makeup.

Me: Lol love it. And yes, I'm all of those things...100%. Hoping you're asleep on the plane.

Andrew: [several hours later] Finally here in Dubai.

OYSTERS

my crazy #1

During Andrew's week-long Dubai trip, we stay in constant contact. We stay in such close contact that I almost don't believe he's there. Given the time difference, it seems he practically never sleeps. My inner sleuth convinces me to at least verify the flight times he told me – and luckily for him, everything checks out. Sure, he could've just looked up Orlando-to-Dubai flight times, but that just seems like way too much to go through, so I believe (for the most part) that he really went.

my crazy #11

Though it has only been a week, Andrew and I have talked so much that when another guy I met recently, Rich, reaches out because he's in town from D.C. and wants to go on a date the night before Andrew returns, I actually feel guilty taking him up on the offer. *It's strange. How do I feel like I'm committed to Andrew after only one week?* I know I'm very much able to date someone else, though I don't feel it emotionally. So, I decide to go on the date with Rich, and I don't tell Andrew about it – I have no obligation to. Besides, I'm pretty sure I don't like Rich; I'm only trying to be nice and show him a good time in my city.

On the date, Rich and I share raw oysters (I appreciate that he likes this special delicacy), and all I do is talk about Andrew – partly to put up a wall between Rich and me because I know I'm not interested in him and partly because Andrew has consumed my thoughts. After my date with Rich, despite my pulling back, he posts our dinner photo on Facebook (fortunately Andrew isn't on fb). Rich continues to show interest, telling me he wishes Andrew and me "a bad date" the next night.

Andrew, none the wiser, texts me from Dubai to make plans for our Friday night date back in Orlando.

Andrew: What do you like to eat?

Me: Ha, I eat everything, seafood, sushi, Mexican, Italian… I had a place in mind to take you here Fri but will depend on your flight schedule. I'm flexible after work around 5:30p. Are you staying at the Airport Marriott again when you land?

Andrew: I will be at the Ritz.

Awesome, I think to myself. *There goes that great luxury taste again. I won't complain about that.*

Me: Oh, the Ritz is virtually walking distance from my job, so having dinner near your hotel works even better for a Friday evening date.

turn on #5

On his flight home, Andrew emails me from the sky letting me know he made a 7:00 dinner reservation and that the location would be a surprise. This is impressive! I thought I'd have to make dinner arrangements since he had been traveling and he would be in my city. Although I'm not a big fan of surprises (some say I like to be in control, but I like to think that I just don't like when people go out of their way for me 😊), I do appreciate that he took care of the dinner plans.

I call Andrew as I pull up to the Ritz. "Well, hello there," I say sensually, given it has been a week since I last heard his voice.

"Hey, Mimi. How was your day?" he asks.

"Better now. I'm actually pulling up to your hotel," I say smiling and ripping a roller out of my hair.

"Oh, great. Hey, listen, I have a suit on because I want to stop by Mango's later if that's okay with you?" Andrew asks.

"Oh, sure! And I always love a man in a suit!" I respond.

"Ok, and one other thing: do you want to leave your car here and we can take my car? Especially since we'll be making two stops now to dinner and Mango's?"

my crazy #2

Hmmm... ok, insert decision point. I've only known this guy for a week. While I'd love to be in the passenger seat for a change, it wouldn't be wise for me to get in his car since I barely know him. Total stranger danger. Plus, I figure he has some run-of-the-mill low-budget airport rental car anyway. "You know, we just met. I should probably play it safe and drive separately," I say as I pull up to Ritz valet. Andrew is walking toward my car, and I'm fumbling to put on my heels since I drive in flats. I get out the car to hug my date, who is dressed in a nice black suit with a white shirt and no tie. He definitely looks great.

"Heyyyy," I say, giving him a big hug. "Welcome back."

"Thank you, Mimi. It's been a long flight, and I barely slept, but I'm ready for dinner. You ready to get going?"

"Sure thing!" I respond. Andrew tells me we're heading to Eddie V's, and I'm happy since I love it there. He picked the perfect place for our first full date. "You can follow me in your car," I tell him.

Andrew walks to his car, which is already up at valet, and I drive around to meet him. *Uh, wait a minute, whose car is he getting into? What kind of car is that?* I ask myself as I pull up closer behind his rental to see the emblem. *Omg, it's hot. But wait, why on Earth does this man have a Maserati when he doesn't live here?* I'm so confused. I text a few girlfriends something like, 'Uh, who am I out with?' My friend Dina responds that luxury cars like a Maserati can be rented from the airport. Who knew? I decide I'll ask him about his luxury car rental later, but for now, we'll head to Eddie V's.

The waitress seats us comfortably in a booth facing the bar and next to the live jazz band. We sit next to each other in the booth.

Over dinner, we re-cap his Dubai trip. "How did you like it?" I ask as he flips through photos on his iPhone.

"Oh, it was really nice, but I need to go back. We spent so much time working; I barely had time for sightseeing."

my crazy #1

"Oh, I'm sure," I say as I intentionally look at his phone photos for concrete proof that he was actually in Dubai. I know, it's my jaded past that has me not trusting basic information like a man taking a business trip, but I just have to verify what he has told me. When I see the date and location stamp of his photos validating his Emirates travels, along with a couple photos of him at Dubai landmarks that couldn't be photoshopped, I let go of my concerns that I might be out for dinner with an untrustworthy person. I begin to believe I am out with a great guy who is going out of his way to have dinner with me at a pretty pricey restaurant after a long flight.

We share raw oysters just like I had the night before with Rich – oops! And I have the lemon sole since Andrew insists I order a full meal. I would usually order only a salad to be a nice, cheap date and because it's almost 8:00. I'm glad I order the sole, though, because it is quite yummy.

I finish my second glass of Sauvignon blanc when Andrew's phone rings. "Mimi, I need to grab this. It's my boss." I motion that I am perfectly fine with him taking the call. I overhear Andrew assuring his boss that we will meet him at Mango's in about 20 minutes. "Ok, Will, see you then," Andrew says before hanging up.

Before I know it, dinner is over and we're out at Eddie V's valet, where I'm faced with yet another decision. "Mimi, since Mango's is just down the street, and we'll have to valet there too, do you want to take one car?" Andrew asks.

my crazy #2

Oh, boy. Well, luckily, I know I have a couple friends going to Mango's tonight, so I can text them to make sure they look out for me. Plus, my inner cheap girl wants to save the $15 Mango's valet money. And that dang curiosity of mine wants to see the inside of a Maserati... H*ll, blame it on the alcohol, I'm sold. "Ok, sure, we can leave my car here, and I can ride with you."

I get in the Maserati and am pretty impressed. I see the rental car company key and I have to know. "So, uh, what made you rent a Maserati?" I ask, pointing him in the direction of Mango's, which is only five minutes away.

Calmly, Andrew replies, "I'm most comfortable driving what I have at home."

Well, alright. That takes care of any thoughts that he rented this car just to impress me while driving a Saturn back in Vegas. (Another guy I recently went on one date with drives a Saturn, so let's just say the Mas is a step in the right direction.) Also, since his company is paying for the rental, I certainly can't complain about him being wasteful with his money.

We pull up to Mango's and walk in. It's dark, loud, and crowded like one would expect on a Friday night. He immediately sees his boss, Will, who he had spoken to earlier. Andrew asks me to excuse him while he goes over to check in with him. I sit on the bench in the club's entryway, looking down at my phone to see if my girlfriends have arrived yet. Within a minute, Andrew and his boss walk over to me. "Mimi, I want you to meet my boss, Will," Andrew says.

It's like something out of a movie. Is this the same Will who I met a few months ago at a party? It's dark in the club, so I look at Will more closely and I see the way he is looking back at me - guilty yet conniving. *Yup, it's him*. I found out not long after I met Will at a party that he is married with three kids, but that didn't stop him from asking me out. Thankfully, I was smart enough to do my research and decline. Wow, just my luck.

"Oh, hey, Will," I say to him, extending my hand and returning a confident "I got you, sucker" smile.

"Oh, wow, the two of you know each other?" Andrew asks with surprise in his voice.

Laughing at the irony and awkwardness of it all, I reply, "Yeah, I know a few people around town."

Andrew says goodbye to his boss shortly after my introduction, and we head upstairs to Mango's dance room, where we first met a week prior. Once we're out of Will's earshot, I let Andrew know what's going on. "So, uh, your boss and I met a few months ago. I'm not sure how to tell you this, but...he asked me out," I say.

Laughing, Andrew responds, "You know, Mimi, I'm not surprised. I know how he is, and please don't share this," he whispers, "but I know he has hired escorts in the past."

Good grief! So, this man is not just a cheater, but he actually hires women - what a class act 🙄. Thank goodness I knew better than to get tangled up with this advanced cheater. I show Andrew text messages that Will had sent me previously just to make sure

turn on #6

Andrew has all the information and can see how I had severed contact with Will once I knew what he was about. And actually, seeing Andrew's disgust for his unfaithful boss makes me trust him even more.

Twenty minutes later, as luck would have it, we run into Will again – this time with his wife. *Great*. I shake her hand, trying not to let my feelings toward her cheating husband show on my face. I feel awful for her, and at the same time I wonder if she knows how her husband behaves. Maybe she stays in the relationship for the kids or for financial security. I'll never know.

Andrew and I walk over to the bar to order their infamous mojitos. Standing there, listening to the hip-hop music with his arm around me, Andrew whispers, "Can I kiss you?" Without hesitation, I turn and allow my eyes to tell him yes. There are no crazy fireworks, no insane passion, but I'm turned on, nonetheless.

We proceed to have a great night together, dancing and laughing, and he even gets to meet my friends Alia and Leila. Leila doesn't think Andrew is my type – he's a big guy and he looks older than 39, so I understand. But everyone knows I can look past unappealing physical attributes and be with someone who treats me well, and so far, Andrew is doing just that by taking me out for a nice dinner, introducing me to his boss, and carving out time for me after an intense week in Dubai.

Andrew walks downstairs to check in with his boss again. Meanwhile, I go hang out with Leila, who looks like she just met a new guy over by the bar. "Mimi, let me introduce you to Rod. Oh, and that's his friend Harper over there," she says, pointing across the room to a tall and very attractive guy who I had noticed earlier.

"Nice to meet you," I say, acknowledging her new friend Rod.

Leila pulls me aside and whispers, "So, what do you think of Harper? He wants to meet you."

my crazy #3

Well, here's another conundrum, I think to myself. I'm here on a date with Andrew, things are going well, and I'd hate for him to walk back in and see me talking to another guy – especially a guy who looks as good as Harper. He is the epitome of tall, dark and handsome. He looks like a basketball player – 6'5", in impeccable shape with runway model looks. I thought I felt Harper staring at me earlier, but I tried to ignore it since I'm out with Andrew.

Next thing I know, Harper has walked over and is standing next to me. "I didn't get your name," he mentions.

Sugar. All I need is for Andrew to walk in right now and see me talking to this hot man. "Hi, I'm Mimi," I say, still contemplating how to get out of this situation.

"Nice to meet you, Mimi. So, you're friends with Leila? Do you live here too?" Harper asks.

"I do. How about you?" I ask, trying to be nice. Plus, I am genuinely curious since I have never seen him around.

"I live in New York. I'm only in town for a few nights for a conference," the hottie says.

"Oh, I see." I'm carefully watching the door in case Andrew returns.

"So, do you think you'd have time for dinner or something before I leave in a few days?" Harper asks.

my crazy #11

Goodness, I am so torn. I have known Andrew for only a week, so I have no commitment to him, but I'm on a date with him. Could I give my number to another guy? I quickly take Harper's phone, which is in his hand, and I enter my number. "My weekend

21

is pretty busy, but we can try and figure something out," I respond, feeling somewhat guilty but rationalizing that I don't want to deny myself an opportunity because of someone I've known only a week, no matter how good things are with Andrew. I tell Harper I'm here with someone else – which he knew – and so I have to go.

I walk back toward the dance room entrance to wait for Andrew, still feeling Harper's eyes on me. I sit to watch Alia salsa dance nearby and resist the urge to look back in Harper's direction. When Andrew finally returns, we dance a little more before saying goodbye to my friends and to his co-workers (thankfully, there is no sign of boss Will and his wife), and we head out to his car.

"I had a really great time tonight, Andrew. I'm glad we came back to Mango's. It was like a one-week anniversary," I say jokingly.

"Yes, luckily I didn't have to work much tonight, and we were able to enjoy ourselves," he says.

We're driving back to get my car from our dinner location at Eddie

turn on #3

V's. "So, Mimi, I actually brought you back something from Dubai – it's at the hotel. I meant to bring it for you earlier, but it was in my co-worker's room and he wasn't there when you arrived," Andrew says.

Hmm... for a minute, I wonder if this is just Andrew's way of luring me back to the Ritz for a nightcap. But I feel that he is such a gentleman, and it seems like he's being sincere. Besides, all I have to do is pull up to valet – there is no obligation for me to go to his room. "Ok, I can follow you back to the hotel," I respond.

turn on #7

We pull up to the Ritz, and his co-worker is waiting at valet with the gift bag for me. Opening the gifts, I find chocolates, a Dubai magnet (which I told him I collect) and a Burj Khalifa picture frame which I totally needed, though he didn't know it. "This is so thoughtful, Andrew. Thank you so much!" I say. I can barely believe that this almost perfect stranger is kind enough to bring me back souvenirs from his trip overseas. I drive home feeling pretty high.

turn on #2

Back at the house, after a great Friday evening with Andrew and the bonus of meeting another guy, I receive text messages from both to make sure I got home okay (nice job, gentlemen). Harper also confirms that I'm up for a date the next evening. I have a gala to attend, so I can't do dinner as he suggests, but I offer to meet him for a drink after my gala. I tell him that, as we just met, I'd prefer if Leila and Rod came too.

BACON

turn off #1

The next day, Andrew had to fly back home to Las Vegas. He texts me, 'Your all I thought about on the plane. I'm going to change a few flights around next month and come back if you want to hang out again? I didn't know if I'd get a second date.'

He's playing coy, and it is cute – except for his "your/you're" misspelling once again ☺. I let him know that I can't wait for him to return. I then go to a golf tournament and gala. I text Andrew pictures and continue our frequent communication throughout the day.

Later that night, after the gala, I go to meet Harper, along with Leila and Rod, for a drink at Vines. On my way there, Harper texts me, 'What would you like to drink upon arrival?'

'Wow, you're awesome. I'll take a glass of Pinot Noir please?' I text back.

When I arrive, Harper looks just as good as I remembered. As we sit at the bar, sharing a calamari appetizer and the bar's legendary free bacon, I learn that Harper has two children and has been divorced twice. Before I know it, Harper has one arm around me and another hand on my thigh. He's very touchy-feely, and while I appreciate the interest, I surely feel it is a bit too much too soon. Other friends from the gala are arriving at this preferred after-hours spot to see me with Harper's arms wrapped around me like the squid we were eating, and I'm sure they're thinking, 'Hmmm, who is that with Mimi?'

But Harper just won't let go. "Mimi, I just can't get enough of you," he says as his hand moves further up my thigh, under my black pleather dress that I had changed into after the gala. Good thing I took off my Spanx. "How about we get out of here and you come back to my room so we can relax and have some fun?" Harper says.

Wow, really, dude? I guess that's what happens with hot guys who are used to getting whatever they want from ladies. "Harper," I say looking him straight in the eye, "that's not going to happen." I feel instantly disappointed that this cute guy has quickly turned into a total loser.

"Well, how about we just go into the bathroom in the back?"

Is this guy out of his mind? I turn to Leila, who had arrived not long before my prince turned into a toad. "I have to get going. This guy is a freak!" I whisper to her without going into too much detail since he's still sitting next to me. Turning back to my toad, I say, "I need to get going, Harper," while trying to stay calm.

"Well, let me walk you to your car. It's raining," Harper offers. I oblige but quickly regret allowing him to walk me when he asks, "Can I just get in the car with you for a minute? It's cold and wet out here."

This guy is relentless. I don't get it. I'm still convinced that I somehow look like an easy target. "Harper, that's not a good idea. I'm going home."

Andrew has been texting me while I was out with Harper, so I'm happy to call him on my way home and talk to a real gentleman.

"I know we've only known each other for a couple weeks, Mimi, but I want to see how you're feeling about us," he says. Wow. I'm feeling a little guilty given that I'm coming off a date with another guy 😳.

"Well, I like you a lot, Andrew. I'm looking forward to seeing you when you're back in town," I reply.

"That's good to hear. Listen, I want to let you know that I'm not seeing anyone else, and while I do have female friends that I take to clubs with me so that they can enjoy Vegas nightlife for free, I'm not dating any of them, and I just want to be honest with you so you can feel comfortable about us."

So, here I am, picking up another guy on my last date with Andrew at Mango's, while Andrew couldn't be kinder or make himself more available to me. I decide at this point that no one else is worth jeopardizing what Andrew and I are establishing, no matter how early it is. Though I receive a few more text invites from both Harper and Rich over the next couple weeks, they eventually disappear after I reject their offers to talk or meet up again. And seeing the contrast between a jerk like Harper and a gentleman like Andrew only pushes me closer towards Andrew.

CHOCOLATE

Over the next two months while we're apart, Andrew and I stay in continuous contact via text and phone calls. He's there for me emotionally when my mom is admitted to the ER and unable to breathe from her pneumonia. He even offers to fly from Vegas to Orlando to be by my side. Despite the three-hour time difference and his schedule that requires him to work late nights at Vegas clubs, Andrew is very responsive, and he constantly reaffirms his feelings for me, always saying things like "miss you," "thinking of you," and "I like you so much." He calls me at work virtually every day to say hello. He even sends me a gorgeous bouquet of flowers in a Lenox vase to my office with a note saying that he "L's" me – code for something just short of loving me. He sends a second set of flowers for Valentine's Day – six weeks in to knowing me, this time with an "L-O." I am overwhelmed and on an emotional high. I text him.

> **Me:** It feels unreal to have met someone with a big heart who is respectful and who I trust. I can hardly believe this…

> **Andrew:** Lol I think it's the other way around. I mentioned to you that you make a guy want to be better. It's like I want to tell you everything I'm thinking but I'm afraid to, well not afraid but I guess guarded which I need to work on. Excited about seeing you soon.

Andrew even offers to contribute to my annual charity event for homeless women. And even though he doesn't end up contributing free beverages as intended, I believe he really wanted to and just ran out of time.

In addition to being there for me and being quite generous by sending "just because" flowers, our conversations get a little more than flirtatious.

turn off #1

> **Andrew:** Your like chocolate and I'm becoming addicted.

> **Me:** *sending kisses* (trying to ignore the fact that, at this point, he clearly does not know how to spell 'you're').

> **Andrew:** I have got to say one thing to get it off of my mind – I want you so bad.

> **Me:** The feeling is 100% mutual. ☺

Andrew: I don't usually say that, but you do something to me.

Me: Good… That's the way it should be. *kisses*

Andrew: If I was with you right now, I would kiss you from head to toe and not miss a spot. I would take my time and explore, and my tongue would… Well I'll stop so I don't offend you. I'm so hard right now.

Me: Killin me babe, killin me! *kiss kiss*

There were times when I thought Andrew was a little too good to be true, like when he'd text me, 'How is the most beautiful woman in the world doing this morning?' or when he said he told his mom that he's head-over-heels for me.

my crazy #4

One morning, Andrew texts me "good morning." Feeling the need to validate his honesty, I call him immediately – partly to investigate whether he can answer a call from me without any notice. He's in a hotel for work and, yes, part of me wants to validate that he is there alone, but I also just want to hear his voice 😊.

intuition alarm #10

When I call Andrew right after he texts, he doesn't answer. He calls me back about five minutes later, saying he had his phone on silent. My instinct tells me he's not being fully honest. Something just doesn't sit right with me, especially when he doesn't stay on the phone with me long. But without any hard reason to believe he's with someone else, I blame my distrust on the man-bashing Lifetime movie I just watched.

intuition alarm #10

There are a couple other questions that pop in my mind. For instance, when I connected with Andrew on LinkedIn, his profile photo looked like that of a used-car-salesman. In addition to that, his LinkedIn timeline showed that he started working in

1993, which didn't align with his age of 39. As questionable as it all is, I choose to believe he is genuine. So, I put those questions out of my mind because he seems amazing in so many ways.

Andrew and I try to plan trips to see each other in the two months between January and March, but our schedules don't align. We also try to Skype but only make that happen once, primarily due to the three-hour time difference. So, needless to say, when Andrew finally returns in early March, seeing each other again is long overdue.

STEAK

Speeding down Narcoossee Road to meet Andrew for a Thursday night dinner at a new trendy local restaurant, 310 Lake Nona, I'm filled with nervousness once again. Am I about to reunite with the proverbial prince charming that I didn't think existed? He seems to be doing almost everything just right.

Fumbling to put on my red high heels, I see Andrew walking toward me. We had pulled up to the restaurant at the exact same time. I get out of the car to give him a huge hug. "I can't believe you're here," I say warmly yet still feeling nervous. He gives me a quick kiss on the lips even though neither of us is one for PDA. Plus, I'm only minutes from my house, so I don't want to be caught making out in the parking lot ☺. Andrew is in a suit – again. I'm not sure how he travels so dressed up all the time, but I'm not complaining. His warm smile and calm demeanor help to mellow me some and bring me back to reality because it does feel like a dream seeing him for the first time in two months.

"Shall we?" he says, extending his arm to escort me in for dinner.

turn on #5

"Good evening. Henlon, party of two?" Andrew says to the hostess. He did it again – earlier, when he was flying in, he had emailed me the OpenTable dinner reservation he made from the sky at the restaurant I had picked. I love that he took the lead once again.

"Right this way," the hostess says as she escorts us to a cozy booth by the bar.

I want us to sit next to each other in the booth like we did on our first date at Eddie V's, but we play it cool and sit on opposite sides. We have the whole weekend to spend together anyway. I sit down in the booth, and for the next 20 seconds or so, time seems to stand still. Andrew, still standing, removes his sports coat, almost in slow motion, and turns to hang it on a hook... Well... I feel like he must've swallowed a bus since the last time I saw him, omg. Seeing him do a full 360 as he turns to hang up his jacket, I think to myself, *Is he really THAT big? Yikes.* I pride myself on not taking issue with physical appearance, but wow, seeing his stomach for the first time, up close and personal, with just a white button-up shirt on, I wonder if I can 'stomach' a man **this** big.

I really don't hear much of what Andrew says over dinner because I'm just looking at him trying to process it all. *Is THIS the man of my dreams?* Not that I ever dreamed of having a man because it's not really who I am – I've never had the fairytale "happily ever after" image in my head. But I guess, better stated, is this my best and final? Will my FOBO (fear of better options) kick-in if I date someone I'm not fully attracted to? Then I remind myself of the phrase etched on a journal I had recently received from my friend Joy, who has been married for 20 years: 'It's what's on the inside that counts.' I had been writing about Andrew in the journal since the day we met, and reflecting on that phrase, about what's on the inside, I try to clear my thoughts of never being able to fully wrap my legs around this huge man.

"So, Mimi, you know I don't want the night to end this soon, right?" Andrew says, stuffing a piece of steak into his mouth and jolting me from the daydream – or should I say nightmare – I'm having about him. He isn't a messy eater by any means, but at this point, everything he puts in his mouth just makes me want to take it out.

"Uh, right, me neither. It's still pretty early," I respond, looking at the time on my phone and trying to shake off my negative thoughts about his size.

"I promised not to keep you out too late, but what if you leave your car here and we go back to my hotel to spend some more time together? I have a conference call to take, but I just want to be in your presence," Andrew says in the most innocent way possible.

my crazy #2

It *is* only 9:00 on a Thursday night, so I don't mind staying out a little longer. But I'm not sure if I'm comfortable going to his hotel since this is only our second time really being together. I rationalize it by telling myself we've been talking for two months, and I'd tell my friends where I am going. Also, there are cameras and security at the hotel (assuming he doesn't rob me on the way there lol), so it is safer than other options, like going to a man's house on the second date. "Ok, we can go to your hotel, but only for about an hour. I need to get home by 11:00 so I'm not too tired for work tomorrow," I respond with a smile.

Andrew had rented a huge black Infiniti seven-passenger SUV from the airport for the weekend – it definitely suits his linebacker body size. I text my friends to let them know where I'm heading.

Up in Andrew's room, he removes his jacket once again, and I take another look to confirm what I had seen earlier – *Yup, he's still huge*. If anything, in the brighter hotel room light, I'm even more alarmed.

"Babe, I'm going to jump on a video conference call, but just make yourself comfortable," he says, once again jolting me back to reality.

I stretch out across the bed and proceed to text my friends, letting them know I'm okay.

Andrew mutes his call. "Babe, I meant to tell you, I grabbed these magazines for you at the airport earlier. I thought you might want to pick out a vacation spot for us," he says, pointing to a copy of Condé Nast on the nightstand. Well, he's speaking my language. Feeling bad about fat-shaming Andrew in my head, I flip through the magazine and try to envision us taking a fabulous vacation together one day – that would be nice. Maybe I'll just have to cancel the vision of him in a Speedo with six-pack abs – it's more likely that I'll see him just carrying a six-pack of beer.

After Andrew finishes his video call, I motion for him to join me on the bed. He lays down on his back, with his shirt, pants and belt still on – he seems nervous. He doesn't touch me, and I appreciate him being a gentleman, but I have to know how being physical is going to work. I wrap my arm around him and kiss him. He stays stationary on his back. *Well, this is different.*

"Mimi, I really want to take things slow. I don't want to ruin what we have," Andrew says.

Interesting! This is new for me, but I definitely can't argue with it.

After laying in Andrew's comfy hotel bed and talking for about 20 minutes, we get up, and Andrew takes me back to my car. We never really made it past first base, which somewhat makes sense given that we have the whole weekend together – there'll be plenty of time to turn it up a notch.

SPINACH DIP

The next day, Andrew and I meet for lunch because my office and his company's Orlando office happen to be in the same corporate complex – just another sign, it seems. We grab lunch outside on the nearby Ritz golf course. It is a gorgeous, sunny 75-degree March day with a breeze.

"So, what part of Orlando would be the best place to live if I were to get a place here?" Andrew asks. This isn't the first time we've talked about Andrew moving here for me, but I'm glad he seems to really want to do it since he is bringing it up. I give him a few suggestions as we enjoy our brief lunch hour together.

After work, it's Friday evening, and I'm ready for the weekend with Andrew. We made plans to see the Orlando Magic game Friday night, go to the spa on Saturday afternoon, to a gala Saturday night, and then to Discovery Cove on Sunday. Before we head to his hotel to get ready for the Magic game, we meet up at a nearby Publix and liquor store along the way. It turns out that Andrew and I even have the same favorite mixed drink taste: Peach Ciroc and cranberry juice.

Sipping on our cocktails and eating Publix sushi rolls back in his hotel room, I finally remember to ask Andrew for his driver's license. I'm spending a lot of time alone with this man and really don't have any proof that he is who he says he is, outside of knowing his boss, who isn't a good person.

intuition
alarm #1

Searching through his wallet for his license, Andrew says, "Hmmm, that's strange. I don't see my ID. You know what? The rental car agent must have put it back in the envelope with the rental car agreement. Remind me when we get to the car to grab it."

"Oh my, yes, sure, you'll definitely need to get it out of the car," I respond. Well, a couple of glasses of Ciroc later, I'm exhausted. The thought of riding downtown, parking, walking, and going to a basketball game feels like too much. Fortunately, Andrew is feeling the same way, and we decide to take a nap instead of going to the game. But, like the night before, we remain at first base in bed.

I wake up and get ready to head home around 11:00 p.m. We had decided it was too soon for an overnight date. Andrew showers to go out to Mango's for work, and though he does invite me, I'm too tired to join him.

After I get home, I text Andrew to remind him about his driver's license before I fall asleep, but he never texts back about it, and I forget about it by the time I wake up Saturday.

Saturday morning at 8:00 a.m., Andrew comes to my house for the first time to pick me up for the day. I live out of the way, but I'm glad he's such a gentleman and wants to chauffeur me around. My parents are in town at my house and Andrew had hinted the night before about wanting to meet them, but I think it's too soon, so I don't push it.

"This is such a nice area," Andrew remarks as we drive through my neighborhood back to the expressway. "Are there any new homes for sale nearby?"

intuition
alarm #2

Wow, he wants to look at homes? This is somewhat of a good sign. But his suggestion gives me a flashback of the last time I looked at houses with a guy I had only known a couple months (it was the guy I met at City Walk and drove to his hotel that time – I now refer to him as "Cali.") One month in, he promised to move from California to Orlando for me. That, of course, never happened after I discovered he was a pathological liar. So, the thought of going down the house-hunting path again with a guy I've only known a couple months rings an alarm, but I don't want to project prior bad experiences onto Andrew. He seems like a really good guy.

"Well, actually, there's a new home community a couple lights up from here. We could drive around the community if you just want to get a feel for what's in this area," I suggest. Andrew agrees.

I figure we'll just drive around the community. However, after we pull up, Andrew insists that we not only get out of the car but that we go into a house. The house is under construction with danger signs and warning tape all over it. Luckily, I notice no one is around as we approach the shell of a house.

"So, what do you think? Is this something you would like?" Andrew asks me, standing on a piece of cardboard covered in sawdust.

"Sure, I love the grand staircase and the open concept," I say hesitantly, still haunted by the doomed luxury-house-hunt I experienced previously with Cali years prior and at the same time hoping no one sees us peeping around the house. Thankfully, we exit with no issue.

We jump back in the car and head to the Ritz for our spa appointment. I had booked a couple's massage to treat Andrew because he had never had a massage and I feel he has been great to me over the past couple months.

"Checking in under Mimi Mansfield?" I say to the spa front desk attendant.

"Oh, yes, we have you listed for a hot stone couple's massage, Ms. Mansfield?" the attendant responds.

"Yes, that is correct," I confirm.

"Ok, great. Here are your locker keys, and you can follow me up to the locker rooms."

Andrew and I change into our robes in the separate changing rooms. We meet in the private couple's massage room after.

"Ok, you'll want to get fully undressed and lie face-down under the sheet," one of the two masseuses instructs as they leave the room and close the door.

Well, here is another moment of truth – seeing Andrew naked – and I'm not sure I want to. Well, we're both pretty sheepish and don't want the moment to turn into a striptease, so we both duck and dive behind our respective massage tables, robes, and sheets. Thankfully, Andrew spares me, and all I see is a very brief flash of pasty pale skin diving under a white sheet. I put the image out of my head and try to relax.

"You ready for your first massage?!" I ask Andrew.

"Well, I'm a little nervous, but I'm sure this is something I need in my life."

Knock, Knock.

"Yes, we are ready. You can come back in," I say to the masseuses.

We both drift off to sleep some during the massage – must've been the dim light and strong scent of lavender that filled the room. I can hear Andrew snoring, and while I'm glad he's relaxing for a change, I'm also thinking about the $150 I spent on his massage, and I know he needs to wake up to get the most out of it. But over-all, I'm happy to do something nice for him; it makes me feel good. When his masseuse flips him over, I hear him awaken, and before I know it, our moment of serenity is broken.

"Ok you two, you're all set. I hope you enjoyed your treatments," says one of the masseuses.

"Yes, that was great," Andrew responds groggily. "I need to do this again soon." I'm certainly pleased he enjoyed the massage.

We stumble outside to the spa's private pool, still in a state of ultimate relaxation.

We order light food and drinks and proceed to continue getting to know each other. "So, you played football in college?" I ask, spooning out our spinach dip appetizer.

"I played at Oklahoma State until I got injured in my sophomore year – I tore my ACL. It was awful," Andrew responds.

"I bet it was," I say with sadness.

"Because of my injury, I transferred schools to be closer to my family back in Texas. The goal was to recover. However, I never played sports again," Andrew shares. "But you know, those couple of years in Oklahoma were some of the best. When I would travel with my teammates, we would tell people we were going to the NFL, and they would give us anything we wanted," Andrew exclaimed, almost like he was reliving his college glory days in front of me.

"That's crazy!" I respond, enjoying seeing his face light up while he reminisces. I ask Andrew, "So, you asked me before what is one thing about me that people would be surprised about. What would be your answer? What would surprise me about you?"

"That I really loved Prince as a kid, and I would choreograph dances to his music in high school."

"Wow!" I respond. Now that is an image for sure.

The sun is starting to set on our relaxing spa-and-pool day. We need to head back inside to the hotel room and get ready for the gala. Conveniently, each of our jobs offered us tickets to the Orlando Magic Youth Foundation gala, and we have planned to go together.

Walking up to the Amway Arena, Andrew sees a co-worker of his and introduces me. We take a photo together on the "step-and-repeat," and once inside, we head to our respective company tables for the dinner.

After dinner, Andrew comes to my table to meet my co-worker and friend Jacques as well as my friend Giselle. "It's nice to meet you both," Andrew says. I stand by, somewhat nervously, hoping that my friends will like Andrew.

I step away to let them talk, and when I return, Giselle shares with me, "So, I asked Andrew about his goals for your relationship, and he replied that he just wants to make you happy."

I smile, patting Andrew on the back. "Aww, thanks, babe."

He also talks shop with Jacques – they share a love for fishing. I feel like Andrew has passed another important test: getting the initial approval of my friends.

On the way back to the hotel, my friend Dina texts that she is at Eddie V's and wants to meet Andrew, too. Andrew and I stop by for a quick introduction, and like Giselle, Dina thinks he's a nice guy. "I'm so excited for you guys!" she exclaims.

turn on #3

Back at the hotel, we have another fully clothed night in which Andrew barely tries to make any moves on me. Since I'm not overwhelmingly physically attracted to him, I'm not jumping at the opportunity to get between the sheets, but it is a different experience for a man to be so controlled in the bedroom. I interpret it as Andrew being a true gentleman and I tell myself that this is the way it should be. It only makes me trust him more to know that he isn't out for only a physical relationship with me. Once again, Andrew doesn't encourage me to spend the night and he drives me home at a decent hour.

WINGS

It's Sunday and our last full day together during this visit. The plan is to treat Andrew to a resort called Discovery Cove, where we can swim with dolphins and relax on the sand, right in the middle of Orlando.

Andrew picks me up from my house again, and we head to the resort. As we check in, the attendant asks for ID from both of us to prepare our badges for the day. We each present our licenses directly to the attendant. After checking in, we walk down the pathway to what I consider my local mini-paradise – an experience I am happy to share with Andrew.

"Wow, this is beautiful, Mimi. I never would have guessed this is here," he says.

"Yes, I just love coming here and bringing my friends. I'm glad you're pleased," I say, smiling. We get cozy in our cabana with drinks and take in another gorgeous, sunny 75-degree March afternoon.

Laying in our cabana lounge chairs, I want to learn more about Andrew. "So, tell me about the last person you dated." Though we have spent a few days together at this point and have talked on the phone daily for two months, I still don't feel like I know Andrew **that** well.

"So, there was a woman who was interested in me who lives in Southern California, but we weren't really the right fit," he says.

intuition alarm #3

Once Andrew mentions California, I flash back to our Mango's conversation the first night we met. He mentioned going to California for Christmas. Taking a sip of my champagne, I ask, "Hmmm you mentioned going there for Christmas – was it to visit her?"

I then watch as Andrew's eyes open wide. I read his face to say that he forgot he told me about his California Christmas trip. "Well, actually yes, Mimi. You have a good memory. I did go there to visit her for Christmas, but we're only friends now."

Hmmm, I think to myself, *sounds like there could be more to the story*. But I let it go so we can enjoy the beautiful resort surrounding us. After all, he is the one who proactively told me he isn't dating anyone else when doing so would be completely permissible after only two months. "Why don't we go and enjoy the lazy river?" I propose.

"Ok, sounds great!" Andrew responds, probably happy that I have released him from the past-relationship inquisition.

Andrew and I proceed to have the best time floating through the lazy river together. We're like a happy couple in the beginning of a relationship, in that new, exciting time when there are no barriers or burdens, no stresses or drama, just pure unadulterated fun.

"I love being in the water," Andrew remarks, pulling me in close as we let the lazy river current carry us through.

"Me too. It just relaxes me." I respond, feeling weightless and wrapping my arms around him. We stop and take a photo under the waterfall, and I'm sure every onlooker thinks we are the picture of happiness. We head to the other pool to snorkel with stingrays and other marine life, holding hands under water and exploring together. We really are having a blissful Sunday afternoon.

"Can we go around again?" Andrew asks, almost childlike, and I'm happy to have made his visit so special.

"Of course! Let's go deeper this time and see the sharks!"

Back at the cabana, we have another round of cocktails and ask the attendant to take a photo of us relaxing on beach chairs in the sand. "Say cheese," he says, snapping our photo and handing me back my phone.

"Thanks so much," I respond. Looking at my phone, I have to do a double-take. *Is that Andrew's stomach?* It looks like a sack of potatoes. He had been wearing the resort-provided vest for the day, but from the angle at which the photo was taken, his vest-less belly looks bigger than ever. *Hmmm, I'll have to crop this before sending it to friends and family. Sorry, Andrew.*

After a day in the water, I decide I want to be bad and get wings for dinner. We stop off on the way back to the hotel where we virtually inhale Gator's Dockside wings and recap our fun day together. We're on cloud nine.

Andrew takes me home around 7:00 p.m. so I can get ready for work the next day. "I can't believe the weekend is over already," I say sadly.

"Yes, it flew by," Andrew responds.

Thinking about my work schedule for Monday, I say, "You know, I can probably stop by your hotel tomorrow morning to say goodbye before you leave if you'll have time?"

"Sure, I'd love to see you. I have my regular Monday morning conference call, but I can mute it for the most part," he responds.

"Ok, perfect. I'll plan to come by in the morning before your flight back to Vegas," I say, smiling.

I arrive at Andrew's room Monday morning in a black and white Calvin Klein wrap dress, which I know he will love, and shiny crimson red heels. "Good morning, Mr. Henlon," I whisper as I step into his room. I see he's on his conference call. He hugs me, giving my outfit a thumbs-up as he motions for me to get comfortable.

I sit on the foot of the bed while he paces the room, chiming in on his call when necessary. Once the call is over, Andrew joins me on the bed. "So, Mimi, I don't know how to tell you this, but... there's a good chance that I'll have to take a position in Japan later this year," Andrew says in a serious tone.

My heart sinks a little. He had mentioned over the past couple months that his company has been grooming him for an international position, hence the Dubai trip. And he knew the only way to move up in the company would be to work internationally, but I had not expected a transition this soon. I have to manage my feelings because our relationship is so new. I have zero claims on his future, even though we have been talking as if we're likely to have one together. "Well, that's a good opportunity for you. What do you think you'll do?" I ask.

"I'm really not sure, Mimi. I know it sounds crazy because we just met, but I don't want to lose you."

The morning has taken an unexpectedly emotional turn. "Well, maybe it's something we can work through. I do love to travel, you know," I say, trying to lighten the mood.

"I would keep my house in Las Vegas and be back and forth likely once per quarter," Andrew says, also trying to provide silver linings. We know we don't have all the answers at this point, so we table the discussion. I have to get to my office anyway.

I leave Andrew feeling pretty uncertain about what the future holds. I'm fairly confident that his feelings toward me are genuine, and I believe he will do his best to make things work with us. Andrew even calls me to meet him once more before he leaves Orlando. During this final meeting, I hop back in his big black SUV, and we hold hands while he's on yet another conference call. He kisses me goodbye before heading to the airport. As he does, he says, "Love you" – the full L-word this time – and I return the sentiment.

SUSHI

Though he's back at home in Vegas, Andrew and I resume our frequent communication.

Me: Meant to tell you, I finally caught up with my dad. He said, "I saw your Discovery Cove photos, we'll need to meet this guy, what's his full name?" Told him he can meet you in a few weeks when you come back in town. 😊

Andrew: Sounds good. I told you I want to meet them, and don't forget to send me their favorite drink.

Me: Will do. Btw, just remembered you slipped out of town without sharing something with me…

Andrew: What?

Me: [I text a photo of my driver's license.]

Andrew: Blurry. But babe, just go through my wallet when I get back and it should answer any questions you might have.

intuition
alarm #10

Me: Lol I can't believe I forgot – even when we needed our ID's at Discovery Cove, it didn't occur to me to look at yours. **Only thing that sparked it this morning is I noticed Skype shows you with the wrong birth year - it shows 1975 instead of 1976.**

Andrew: [Shoots back a partial photo of a driver's license that shows only his photo and birthday with the year of 1976.]

Me: *kisses*

I feel bad for questioning Andrew. Later, when we talk on the phone about his Skype account discrepancy, he says he was rushing when setting it up to talk to me and clicked the wrong birth year. It makes sense, so I put it out of my mind. We text some more.

Andrew: Talking to mom and guess who she is asking about.

Me: Awww. *kisses* Hi Mrs. Henlon!

Andrew: Yes

Me: Btw, very moved by what you told your Mom about the next year and a half in your life. I am grateful that we are on the same (unbelievable) page 😊. You can tell her next time you talk to her that I'm looking forward to making you happy for as long as I am able. Love you.

turn off #1

Andrew: I think she knows. Your awesome.

Me: YOU'RE awesome. [Nope, he still hasn't learned how to spell 'you're,' but I love him anyway]

Andrew: YOUR HOT!!!!

Me: Lol

Andrew shares with me that if he moves forward with the Japan position, he would make seeing me a priority when he comes back to the States. I'm feeling more and more confident that we can make things work despite the significant geographical barrier. Plus, it's a good thing I like sushi ☺.

We finally find a good time to Skype a couple weeks after our time together in Orlando. "Hey, babe! It's so good to actually see you," I say, smiling on our Skype video call.

"Same here. I've missed you so much," Andrew says, seated in his kitchen like last time. During our previous Skype call, Andrew (virtually) took me outside to show me his backyard full of Vegas-style greenery, which was really nice. This time, I decide I want to see more of his house because he mentioned doing work on the stairs, and I want to see.

"Andrew, why don't you show me around your house?" I ask. We had talked about me coming to Vegas to visit in the coming months before he goes to Japan, and I definitely want to see how he lives before I fly out there.

"Sure." He takes his laptop around, showing me the living room, dining room, and some of the work he recently had done on the very large, spotless, 3,000-square-foot house.

"Wow, your home looks great, Andrew," I share, really impressed at how nice his house is for a 30-something bachelor. Then Andrew

intuition alarm #4

shows me outside the front of his house where I can see his cars. While I'm expecting to see a Maserati based on his comment that he likes to rent what he drives at home, I instead see a nice white Mercedes. "Oh, I didn't know you have a Mercedes," I comment.

"Yes, I have the sedan here, and then over here," he says, swinging the laptop to the driveway, "I have the Mercedes SUV." Definitely beautiful cars, but I do feel either slightly misled or perhaps I had simply misunderstood him. To not sound materialistic, I just assume he meant that he rents cars similar to what he drives at home (a luxury vehicle) and not that he literally has a Maserati. It definitely seems like he can afford one if he wanted, so again, I put any lingering questions out of my mind.

"So, how about your upstairs? I'd love to see the stairs you're working on and your bedroom!" I say excitedly. He had mentioned having a chandelier in his bedroom, which I really want to see.

intuition
alarm #5

"You know, Mimi, my bedroom is a mess right now. Let me straighten it up and I can show it to you in the morning," Andrew says convincingly. I try to tell him that seeing a messy bedroom is not an issue for me, but he doesn't budge. After we hang up, I think to myself, *So much for a spicy in-bed Skype session.*

The next morning passes by without a mention from Andrew about Skyping. In fact, he's out of the house before he calls me. Somehow, Andrew has a way of distracting me. I never even remember to ask him about Skyping again in his bedroom that day.

A few days later, I realize I can carve out a free weekend, and I call Andrew to propose that I fly to Vegas to spend time with him. It would be better than seeing his bedroom on Skype anyway.

Me: I'm getting the urge to get on a plane this weekend... Wish you were going to be stationary.

Andrew: Gosh babe, this weekend just isn't good. When you come out, I want to have uninterrupted time to spend with you. I have so many work commitments this weekend.

While I understand, I'm pretty disappointed. We've been talking long-distance for over two months, and we have only carved out one weekend together so far. I don't doubt that he works really hard, and we are in constant contact so I don't think he could have anyone else significant in his life, but if this pattern is a sign of things to come, I'm not sure how successful we will be as a couple since such a small amount of in-person quality time doesn't give us much of a foundation to build upon.

intuition alarm #4

Talking to my friend Angie, who is in town for the night and crashing at my place, I start to have reservations about Andrew. As I hear myself describe our relationship to her, something just doesn't feel right. "You know, Ang, I really like him, but there are just some things that aren't adding up for me... and I just don't know... I feel like something could be off," I say. I outline for her the difficulty we're having getting me to Vegas, the fact that he was hesitant to show me his bedroom on Skype, and that he was very guarded in sending me his driver's license – sending me the part that didn't show his address – something I thought about after the fact. Andrew had explained that he's really private and didn't want to send a photo of his full driver's license, but it just doesn't make sense. *If I'm the person he's trying to be with, why would he feel the need to keep his address from me? Especially if I'll be traveling soon to see him.* As I say everything to Angie, I realize that I have to do some work to get to the bottom of things.

I call Andrew to explain my reservations. "Babe, you know you're going to be meeting my parents in a couple weeks, and I don't even

intuition alarm #5

know where you live," I tell him, trying to keep the conversation as light as possible. I hope that this will be easy to resolve.

"When I come back to visit you, we can sit down and talk through everything, ok?" he responds. I feel like he's pushing me off again, albeit in the nicest way possible.

intuition alarm #5

I just can't let it go this time. "Andrew, I am at the point where I'd like us to do background checks on each other. If we are as serious as we say we are, I feel like I want that level of protection before things progress," I say, standing my ground.

"Well, you know I'm heading to Japan this summer, and I have so much on my plate. Can we just wait a couple months?" he asks. It doesn't make sense to me why we can't just do the background checks right away, especially before he meets my parents – a meeting that he suggested. But Andrew always has a way of extinguishing my concerns and shifting the conversation. "Babe, I need to grab this call. Call you back later? Oh, and text me your parents' favorite wine so I can make sure the Ritz has it when we meet."

"Sure," I respond, feeling somewhat deflated but still holding on to the great weekend we spent together in Orlando and his pending trip to visit me next weekend.

I want to trust Andrew, but curiosity keeps getting the best of me. I go back to his LinkedIn page to verify what I looked up when we first met. I read it again: he started working in 1993. It just doesn't add up with his age. That sinking feeling comes rushing back.

As I head out to meet two of my very happily married friends, Mellie and Marie, for dinner, I know I have to tell them the latest with Andrew. While there are plenty of positives to share about Andrew, the negatives are starting to creep in. On my way to meet

intuition alarm #4

them, I call Andrew to put my concerns about his LinkedIn profile to rest. After talking to Andrew, I feel more at ease. He explains that he started interning at PepsiCo in the early 90s when he was in high school because his dad worked there and got him a job when he was very young. Given that both my brother and I were fortunate enough to have similar high school internship opportunities working in corporate America in our teens, it makes sense, and I feel better about Andrew once again.

I am almost glowing as I tell Mellie and Marie about Andrew over dinner. I even tell them about our LinkedIn mishap, to which Marie responds, "Girl, why would he lie about his age by only a few years? I'm sure he's telling you the truth." They are so excited for me, and

I'm hopeful about a future with Andrew, but something is still gnawing at me on the inside.

With all my questioning, Andrew is starting to pull back. He hasn't said "love you" for a few weeks and isn't nearly as flirtatious as he had been. Crazy as it is, one of his favorite, almost daily questions, (What color [panties] are you wearing?) has waned along with the regular terms of endearment such as "babe" and "dear," and the text kisses. He blames it on things picking up at work, but I feel it's something more. I just don't know what it is.

intuition alarm #10

I decide to take matters into my own hands one Saturday afternoon because Andrew is just days from meeting my parents. Luckily, I had talked him into giving me his address earlier in the day, though I still couldn't get him to share his full driver's license. I search Google Earth for the address Andrew gave me, and it pulls up a desert area – no house. He had previously mentioned, when he was doing work on his stairs, that his house is eight years old. There is no way that Google Earth hasn't logged his eight-year-old house. My stomach instantly starts doing flips when I realize that the address he gave me seems to be fake. This is the first red flag that sends me on a mission.

I log into the Whitepages people search feature and pull up everything I can on Andrew Henlon in Las Vegas. In the Whitepages preliminary report, I find a couple listings for him, each with a different birth year, which definitely makes me more uneasy. I know I have to find more information. I pay the $29.95 fee for the full Whitepages report. In the section that shows Andrew's related family members, the first person listed is oddly named Mia, just like me. She has his last name and is around my age – in her late 30s. I can't believe that after three months of conversation, he hasn't mentioned that someone in his family has the same name as me. I also notice that Mia is listed as living at one of his houses, which just seems strange. Additionally, there is a child listed among his top five family members (along with his parents and brother), but I assume the child is a niece or nephew.

I call Andrew right away to clarify what I have found and to calm my nerves, hoping he has a simple answer for who this other Mia is.

His response: "Oh, Mia. I haven't mentioned her to you yet. That's my cousin. My cousin Mia and my other cousin Emily. Years ago, at a family reunion, we agreed to buy property and keep it in the family. You'll meet them one day," he says reassuringly.

"Well, what about your age? One report says you're almost 50 years old!" I say.

intuition
alarm #4

"Mimi, you can find anything online. I could show you a report that says I'm 35 and another that says I'm 55. Those things are never right," he responds.

Well, that's Andrew – he always has a quick and relatively solid answer. Part of me believes him because who can lie that well? So quickly without any preparation – he didn't know I was running a background check on him. Although I had agreed to wait a couple months to pull the report, that changed when his house didn't come up in Google Earth. And I was so focused on Mia, I forgot to ask why his address was a desert. Though I am uneasy with his response that Mia is his cousin, I have no choice but to believe him. I tell myself that we can resolve everything face-to-face when he flies to Orlando in five days.

Three nights later, on a Tuesday, Andrew calls me unexpectedly at around 2:00 a.m., though we had already said good night at around 10:30.

"Mimi, I need to talk to you," Andrew says, sounding very serious.

"Hey. Is everything ok?" I ask, feeling like I'm still dreaming. He often called late due to the time difference and his nightclub work hours, but there is something different about his tone tonight.

"I need you to listen to me, ok? Please, wake up?" he says.

"I'm awake," I respond nervously.

"I don't know how to tell you this, but I haven't been completely honest with you. When you asked the other day who Mia is, I should have told you... she's my wife. But hear me out. I just got off the phone with her, and I told her all about you. She and I have not been together for some time because she cheated on me. With her tennis instructor. I really want to be with you, and I'm sorry I didn't tell you this sooner."

I'm shaking. I'm shocked, even though I was expecting he had been hiding something. Ever since his reluctance to share his driver's license with me became an issue, I felt something was off, and I felt I should consider leaving him alone, but I certainly didn't expect him to have a wife. Finding Mia's name the other day definitely made me feel like she was more than a cousin. But I just don't understand. *Why would he lie?*

"Andrew, I can't believe you would do this to me. Why did you lie?" I ask angrily.

"When I met you, I really didn't expect things to take off like they did. I didn't think I was going to fall for you like this. But I promise you, I have ended things with my wife. I want to make this work with you, Mimi. That's why I didn't try and sleep with you. I wanted to do things the right way," he says, still using a tone that I do not recognize. He's definitely using an alternative sense of logic. In his warped mind, not sleeping with me somehow excuses him from lying about his wife and should make me think he's trying to do right by me.

"How long have you been married?" I ask, just trying to fathom the severity of it all.

"Fifteen years."

I can hardly believe it, but it does explain why he, unlike most people I have dated, provided almost no details about his prior relationships. "And how long have you been separated?" I ask.

"We haven't lived together for a couple years. She stays back in Texas."

"So, you were married for 15 years and you didn't have any children?" I ask skeptically.

"Mia... I have a nine-year-old daughter."

What in the h*ll!?! Is this man psychotic?! Who lies about their child? How did he think this would play out? He couldn't hide a child forever! I remember the child listed in the Whitepages report. "Why would you lie about a child, Andrew? That doesn't make any sense! You had to know I'd eventually find out!"

"Well, I knew you didn't want children..." he responds.

I feel like I am talking to a sociopath. At this point, nothing is salvageable. Even if I could see past the alleged estranged spouse and his failure to tell me about her for three months, there is no way I could ever see past the fact that he didn't mention his child. "Do you at least spend time with your daughter?" I ask, suddenly feeling sorry for this poor child growing up with a father who should probably be in a straitjacket.

"Yes, my wife or my mom brings her over from Texas to see me about once a month. They stay in the other house that I own."

This explanation seems relatively plausible since I talked to him every single night, so I don't believe the wife still lives with him. But because he never showed me his bedroom, I will never really know if his wife lived with him. His wife's name had been listed as living at one of his houses on the background check, and the house that he appeared to live in on Skype was really big and well-decorated, so it's possible that she had lived there recently, even if she doesn't live there now.

"I can't help but think you wouldn't have told me any of this if I hadn't run the background check," I say.

"That's why I wanted you to wait a few months on the background check. I wanted to finalize our divorce. It really is over with her, Mimi," he says.

This man is delusional. "Andrew, it's not your marriage that's the issue. It's that you lied about your marriage and, more importantly, about your daughter! That is unforgivable. There's nothing left here," I say, feeling defeated. "I can't believe you were just a couple days away from meeting my parents. You are one sick person."

"I'm so sorry, Mimi. I'm so sorry," Andrew says, attempting to use his most apologetic voice. To me, he still sounds cold and emotionless. I don't know this person.

After hanging up with Andrew, I'm so angry I can't sleep. I toss and turn in bed for an hour, replaying everything that just happened in my head. *Isn't this the way my life goes? I don't need to count sheep to go to sleep. All I have to do is count all of the wolves in sheep's clothing I've met over the years.*

I decide to Facebook instant message my girls.

Just got off the phone with Andrew. He just decided to let me know (2.5 mos in) that he's separated from a wife he never told me about and he has a 9yr old he also failed to mention... Story of my life! I get that when you first met me you didn't want to scare me away with your baggage, but we could've hung out until your divorce was final, there's no need to lie! Esp when things started progressing, he should've never lied and definitely should've told me wks ago, like when he was here visiting. Lying about having a child is the ultimate... Thankfully we never had sex... that's the only thing he did right. So, in true MiMi format, I'm back living la vita single. I'm glad to know now versus later... Esp when the parental mtg was going to be Sat! Thank goodness I pulled a background check on him, think my questions prompted him to come clean...

Giselle: Holy crap. Asshole. He's too old for that kind of lie. I don't get why he wasn't honest. It was a simple thing to do. Sorry MiMi but I hope you don't let this change your mind about falling in love and having it all. You can.

Laying here in my bed, thinking about what Andrew just revealed, it dawns on me how much money I spent when he visited me. I go from disbelief and disappointment to resentment. I text Andrew:

Me: Do me a favor... You still have my address? To make me whole for what I spent, thinking this was something that it wasn't, please mail me a check for $500. That would cover what I put out for Discovery Cove and the spa as well as for this upcoming weekend.

Andrew: Again, I'm very sorry. I deleted everything after I talked to you, so I no longer have your address. I will leave an envelope for you at the hotel front desk later this week when I get to Orlando.

The next morning, I tell Mom that there will be no Andrew meeting.

"Well, I knew he wasn't the right guy for you when he kept dropping you off and not walking you to the door, seeing you had your hands full with bags. He didn't even get out of the car. But I knew you'd figure it out," Mommy says. She can always make me laugh.

A few days later, feeling like I shouldn't have to go out of my way to get reimbursed for what I spent on Andrew, I call him to bring the check by my job. I know he's still coming in town for business. Thankfully, he obliges, and I meet him in my building's parking lot. As he's getting out of his rented SUV, I see him now for the big, fat (pun intended) liar he is. He looks like a different person. He's still dressed in a nice suit, but everything about him feels fake now. He looks like that slick used-car salesman from his LinkedIn photo.

"Thank you," I say, as he passes me $500 in cash. I get back in my car, as there are no words left to be said. Then, I realize I should still ask for his driver's license, just to put the birth year questions to rest. "Andrew, before you go, let me see your driver's license?" I ask with a direct tone.

intuition alarm #5

"Well, can I take you to dinner one last time tomorrow night, and I can explain everything then?" he says.

I roll my eyes. I can finally see through him. I can feel him once again doing his almost magical pattern of trying to pacify me with something pleasant to distract me from getting to the truth. He just wants to kick his lying can down the road in hopes that I'll never get to the bottom of things. "No, Andrew, this is ridiculous. I want to see your ID now, not tomorrow. You just had your wallet out to give me the cash. I know you have it. Why do you feel the need to continue to lie?"

After I ask a few more times, he finally passes it to me reluctantly. 1973. He had lied by three years. It doesn't make any sense. And because Andrew does look older, I will never know if that's even his true birth year or if he showed me a fake ID. I don't ask any more questions because I know he can't offer me any real answers. I simply laugh. "I have to go, Andrew. Take care," I say as I drive away, leaving Andrew and his fat lies in my rearview.

Later that evening, I look again at the ID Andrew had texted me about a month prior – it is a completely different ID than the one he showed me today, and it doesn't even look like a license at all now that I'm seeing it without my emotional blinders on. The whole situation just makes me queasy.

To add insult to injury, the very next day after "ID-gate" with Andrew, I hear from "oyster-date Rich." Rich had checked on me about a month after our date, and I had told him that things were going well with Andrew and that we were official. Well, now things have obviously changed with Andrew, and Rich sees an in for himself, and so he texts me.

Rich: Wow sorry to hear that things didn't work out doll, that's crazy. That's dumb. Lying ages a person.

Me: Yeah real crazy. Just glad I found out sooner than later.

Rich: Well before you run a background check on me, I divorced in 2010, have an 8-year-old son, and will be 46 in August. Also, right now, I'm in the shower...

[He sends a photo of his soaped-up manhood, totally unsolicited. He tries to initiate a video call to which I don't respond].

Me: Please stop messaging me, that is so disrespectful.

Rich: You're right, my apologies. I'm sorry, I acted out of character for a sec.

Rich continues to try and repair our one-date friendship, but he has reached the point of no return by texting me a photo of him "down-under." Plus, he knows the mini-trauma I was just dealing with due to Andrew's lies. His actions are absolutely unforgivable.

I may never know what kind of sick enjoyment some men get out of playing these types of games. I'll never know if the men I've encountered purposefully played on my emotions or if, like Andrew said, they start off with no intention of having anything serious with me, and they feel trapped as it evolves and can't see an honest way out.

Fortunately, by the time Andrew confessed, I had already lost my trust in him and wasn't as emotionally connected to him as I had been. So, the sting of his words wasn't so painful – I almost expected it in a way. I didn't cry when he told me about his wife, and I somewhat laughed to myself because this just seems to be the story of my life: I meet a guy who seems like the perfect gentleman, seems to have a positive energy and presence, who appears great on paper, but in the end, he's anything but. And to think, Andrew told me that he valued "honesty, even when it hurts." In reality, he was anything but honest – he lied about his wife and daughter and misled me about his owning a Maserati. And I'm now convinced he was never going to help with my charity or arrange for me to meet Pitbull. He had just fed me what he thought I wanted to hear. One-hundred percent insanity.

Take a Page from My Book

Love can make you turn a blind eye to your suspicions. Love can make you ignore your intuition. No matter how great he may seem, check yo' menz! I used to tell girlfriends to do background checks right away upon meeting a guy. With Andrew, I broke my own rule. If you are just meeting someone and don't have mutual friends through which to validate him, do your research! Check him out and don't feel guilty about it. If he pushes back, he may have something to hide. Find out if he's a pathological liar before you invest your heart. And a guy who sex-texts with you so quickly (like Rich) is a complete dog – there are no excuses. Run for your life.

**Unworthy Lying Sack of Potatoes –
Andrew and Me at Discovery Cove**

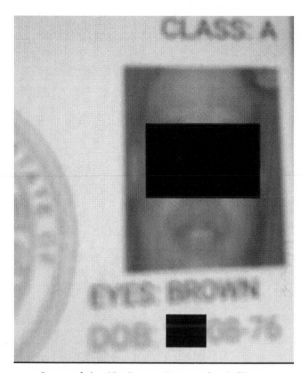

Super-fake ID. Doesn't even look like a
real Nevada license. And, yes, this is all he
sent, partial and blurry. Guess that family
photography business came in handy. 😊

I Should've Left When...

Book of Aruba

DESTINATION: ARUBA

No work stress, no man stress, just the crystal-blue waters of Aruba and a seven-day music festival ahead of me. I'm so ready to vacation and to meet new people. It's been about a month since things went south with married Vegas, so this music festival, which I'm attending with my friend Nadi, has come at the perfect time to help make him a distant memory. Call me Stella.

As Nadi and I are dancing side-by-side at the festival Welcome Celebration, a tall and fairly nice-looking gentleman leans over and whispers in my ear, "What do you know about this music?" He sees me singing and clapping to David Bowie's "Let's Dance." We're looking over the beautiful Hyatt Aruba pool area, watching the crowd dancing and having a good time. The neatly dressed gentleman and I engage in a conversation, and overall, he seems like a good catch. He's professional, 50 years old, has no kids, and seems really interested – but a day later, after going out for dinner and dancing with him, I find myself trying to lose him in the Hyatt resort where we're both staying. He's even driving Nadi crazy, so she coins a name for him: Leech. He does have stalker tendencies and seems to show up (and lingers way too long) everywhere I go at the resort. At one point, he parks himself at the foot of my pool lounge chair and blocks any guy from even looking my way. Thankfully, given that Leech is an "old 50" and therefore can't figure out how to use his smartphone's Wi-Fi (what a turnoff), it should be easy to ditch him on Day 2.

"So, it looks like blindfolded speed dating starts at 2:00 p.m.," Nadi says, reading aloud the Day 2 festival agenda while we get dressed in our room. *Goodness, is this what my life has come to?* Singles events are not my thing, but there's not much else going on at the resort today. Guess it only makes sense to see if there's anyone decent at the resort's speed dating event because Leech needs to be replaced. *sigh*

Even though Nadi and I arrive early to the resort's piano bar for the blind speed dating, we are told that the event is at capacity and that we can't participate (thank goodness), but we can watch – even better. In the cozy, dark, lounge, we sit down on a comfy couch that hugs the wall. It's the perfect spot to watch the speed dating festivities unfold.

"Hey, Nadi! What's up, girl?" says a very round man happily approaching us. He's about 6'3" and easily 300 pounds. His stomach literally wobbles as he walks. He's very out-of-shape, but it doesn't seem to bother him one bit. He actually looks like a darker, fatter version of Vegas.

"Mimi, this is Parker. We used to hang when I lived in D.C.," Nadi says.

"Oh, it's nice to meet you, Parker," I say. As big as Parker is, he somehow squeezes in between Nadi and me on the couch and before I know it, he's asking for my phone number and room number, and he invites us to hang out with him for his chartered flight excursion to Curacao in a couple days. I can tell by the way Parker approached us that confidence is definitely not a problem for him. I suppose his success as a former professional football player helps him feel like he can have any woman he wants despite his very rotund build. I am not remotely attracted to Parker. Plus, Nadi calls him out as having a "situation" back at home with the mother of his four young kids. I conclude that Parker can be a good "trip mate" (i.e., acquaintance) but definitely nothing more. I let him know my stance, and we exchange Facebook information to stay in touch while we're at the resort.

Thankfully, someone else I know (my friend, Ray) walks over and saves me from Parker's advances. "Mimi! Hey, how's it going?" he says. Ray is on the trip with 10 of his male friends for a bachelor party – a group of guys over age 45, mostly married. Ray is super cool, though, and I'm happy to see him. But since he's married, I'm wondering why he's at blind speed dating. "I just came down to see what this is all about," Ray explains. "There really isn't anything else going on right now... Oh, and I figured I needed to bring a few of the single fellas." Ray points over by the lounge's piano. I see two of Ray's friends who I already know from Orlando, both of whom are over age 60 and not for me – I actually went out with one of them a couple years ago, not knowing he was 60, and at 36 years old, I just couldn't make the leap.

However, there is a tall, attractive guy next to them who I have never seen before. He's wearing a T-shirt representing that he's part of the bachelor party, so I realize that Ray must know him. "Hey, Ray, who is that?" I ask, pointing to the attractive guy.

"Oh, that's Luke. You haven't met him before?"

"I haven't. What's his story?"

"Oh, Luke? He's single. He actually lives in Orlando, too. You want to meet him?"

Hmmm... Well, I generally prefer to meet someone more casually, but whatever. "Sure, bring him over."

In just a couple minutes, Ray returns with his attractive friend and introduces him. "Mimi, this is Luke."

"Oh, hi. Nice to meet you," I say, still seated on the tufted couch while he towers over me up close. Luke is 6'6" and really good-looking. "And this is Nadi," I say, introducing Luke to my friend. They shake hands. I have to learn more about this guy. "So, wait, you live in Orlando, Ray said?" I ask, still feeling surprised I've never seen him before.

"Yes, I live in the Metro West area," he responds.

"Oh, I see. I just haven't seen you around."

"Yeah, I don't get out too often," We joke a bit about speed dating and how neither of us wanted to participate. But Luke feels somewhat distant and distracted by the dating activity occurring around us. "Well, it was nice meeting you. I'm going to go back over to watch this speed dating thing," Luke says before leaving.

I conclude that Luke isn't interested in me. I'm a little disappointed, but at the same time, I didn't feel a connection because he seemed so distracted. I'm content continuing to people-watch from the comfy couch. Not long after Luke walks away, Nadi and I leave the piano bar to go look for fun at the afternoon day party .

Nadi and I are doing the wobble outside at the pool with the hundreds of people gathered for the day party. It is overcast weather but just right so that we can keep dancing and not break a sweat. We're having a great time dancing with some of the celebrities who are on the island for the festival.

On my way back to the room to change after the day party, it just so happens that I see Luke walking through the crowd. There are almost 2,000 people at the resort for the festival – it's a minor miracle that I'm seeing Luke again just a couple hours after we met at blind speed dating, but I'll take it. I try to make eye contact with Luke, and I feel like he sees me, but at the same time, he almost looks through me. It gives me a somewhat strange feeling. *Is trying to avoid eye contact, or is he blind?* I just brush it off and keep moving. It feels like further confirmation, though, that Luke is just not that into me – but, oh well, his loss.

It's a couple hours after my chance run-in with Luke. Nadi and I are walking through the bright red-velvet-decorated casino that's full of action, and guess who I see? It's Luke again. This time, Luke

my crazy #10

is seated with Ray and a couple other guys at a cocktail table. I decide to go over and say hello instead of just waving, partly because I'm curious to see what the guys are doing for the night and subconsciously because I haven't fully accepted that Luke isn't interested in me. "Evening, gentlemen," I say, smiling, as we walk up to the table.

"Hey, Mimi. Where are you ladies headed looking all nice?" Ray asks. We had transitioned from daytime rompers into nighttime maxi dresses.

"Oh, we're just heading to the Smooth Grooves jazz lounge down the hall," I respond, pointing around the corner.

turn on #1

"That sounds nice. Maybe we'll join you ladies," Luke responds. Well, I thought Luke was a blind mute, and I'm surprised to hear him chime in.

"Well, yes, you should all come. Nadi went by earlier and said tonight's band sounds great," I say.

"Well, good. We'll look for you there. Oh, and I like your dress, Mimi." Luke says to me.

Interesting. I was wondering if Luke would engage with me – I was getting the feeling that he thought he was too good for me, but maybe I pegged him wrong. "Thanks, Luke. Ok, we'll see you all at the jazz lounge," I say as we walk away.

"Girl, he is so cute. I like him for you!" Nadi says excitedly once we're out of earshot. "Yeah, he is cute, but I can't get a read on him yet," I respond as we enter the jazz lounge. I'm fully expecting that the guys won't even show up because they looked pretty comfortable with their cocktails at the casino. But not even five minutes later, while Nadi and I are still looking for seats at the very crowded jazz lounge, I look over my shoulder and see Luke, Ray and their crew coming to meet us – who would've guessed?

The guys chivalrously help us find seats in the crowded jazz lounge. Surprisingly, only Luke sits down with us; the rest of the guys walk off. Nadi gets up to dance, suddenly leaving Luke and I seated alone. I certainly didn't expect one-on-one time with Luke so soon, but hey, no complaints.

caution #3

Luke sits next to me in the booth, as we both face the dancefloor. It feels like he has totally warmed up. His body language is starting to show interest – it's almost like he went from 0 to 60 emotionally in minutes. Maybe it's my fitted dress and those extra L-Bs I lost before the festival.

"So, how is it that you're single, Luke?" I ask, since his guard seems to be down. He's such a good-looking guy, it's hard to believe he's available.

"Well, I'm divorced, and I do have two children. My son is 22, and my daughter is 12," he says.

"Oh, okay," I respond while thinking to myself, *not even a girlfriend to mention? – I'll take it*. And being divorced with two kids is definitely not uncommon for someone in their late 40s. While I prefer to date someone with grown children, my general rule is that a potential partner's children need to be at least double-digit age, so although 12 is young, but it's not like his child is two.

"So, Mimi, what do you like to do in your spare time?" Luke asks.

"Well, I love to travel, especially to festivals like this. This has been great so far, right?"

"Yeah, it has! I enjoy traveling as well. Where was your last trip?" he asks.

"Hmm, I guess it would've been Thailand about a year ago. It was actually a trip I purchased at a charity auction. I'm glad I was able to go and give to a good cause at the same time. How about you? Where was your last trip?" I say, hoping I sounded worldly and giving but not stuffy.

caution #4

"Well, in August, I took a pilgrimage to Israel," he responds, pulling out his phone and flipping through photos. "Here's where I got baptized in the Sea of Galilee." Luke shows me the pictures on his phone nostalgically. "You know, if I ever got married again, I'd want it to be in Jerusalem. It was so beautiful there."

Wow. I did not expect Luke to be such a devout Christian. It would typically be a woman's dream to meet an attractive and faithful man, but knowing my religious views, I know it is best that I set expectations. "Wow, Luke, that's admirable. It sounds like a great experience. I have to tell you, though, while I was raised Christian and at one point was just like you, I'm more spiritual than religious now, so maybe we'd be better off as friends," I respond. I know it sounds abrupt, but if he's interested, I don't want to waste his time.

"Oh, well I'm not into the church like that. I just go on Sundays for the message. I don't talk to anyone, and I don't participate in anything," he says, almost laughing at the religious corner I had painted him into.

"Oh, I see," I respond, thinking maybe we *can* connect on a faith level since it sounds like he's more open than I thought.

"How about we just hang out and see where things go?" he suggests, looking me in the eye for an affirmative answer.

*Goodness, this guy is so d^mn attractive! And he seems to have a fun personality. What the h*ll (no pun intended)?* "Cool, we can hang out. I'm sure we can have fun together," I respond as innocently as possible.

Apparently, the chemistry between us is noticeable from just our basic conversation because Nadi, who had been watching us talk as she danced, is scrambling to take photos. "Oh my gosh, you guys look so cute together!" she says, snapping a photo. I have to admit, we kinda do look good together. I'm not used to dating very attractive guys, so this would be a shift if it goes anywhere.

The live jazz music is picking up, and Luke asks me to dance. *This is my kind of guy.* Just a few months ago, I had spent New Year's Eve with a guy named Mason, who I am very compatible with. However, he did not like to get dressed up, didn't like to go out, and certainly would not dance. That experience just reaffirmed that I need a true extrovert in my life. And not only do I prefer a man who enjoys social outings, but I really want a man to

turn on #8

take me places and show me things. I don't want to always be in the driver's seat when it comes to keeping us entertained. Dancing with Luke, seeing how fun he is, I start to think that he has the kind of personality that I could enjoy.

turn on #1

We decide to head over to the dance party near the resort's lobby area. Luke impresses me again with how much he enjoys dancing, and I especially love that he is a house music fan – which makes sense, as he is originally from D.C.

"So, what did you and Nadi plan to do tomorrow besides attending the Usher concert?" Luke asks as we walk back to our seats for a break from dancing.

"Oh, we plan to take the chartered boat tour to Bonaire and find our way to a more secluded beach to relax," I respond.

"Well, that sounds nice. Maybe my friend Chad and I can join you?" Luke asks.

Nice. Just when I thought Luke's interest may fade as quickly as it grew, it turns out he's looking for a little more than a one-night affair. "Sure, that'd be cool. We can meet in the morning after breakfast maybe and can go from there.".

turn on #3

Luke walks me back to my room at 3:00 a.m. after a long and unexpectedly fun evening. We exchange phone numbers and connect on Facebook. We hug goodnight – and thankfully, he doesn't ask for a kiss (I feel it's too soon). I send him a message once I'm in bed:

Me: Thank you for a great evening. Have a good night.

Luke: It was my pleasure. Speed dating was a success. Looking forward to seeing you tomorrow. Good night.

Me: Yes, speed dating...no blindfolds lol. Definitely looking forward to tmw. Nte!

BON LUKE IN BONAIRE

The next morning, Luke is up by 9:45 a.m. and texts me.

Luke: I'm showered, my bags are packed and I'm ready to go! What time did you want to hook up?

Me: Luv it, you're on it. I can meet you around 10:45.

Luke: Take your time, no hurry.

Sweet. I like a guy who is excited about life and ready to have fun. Plus, Luke has a light-hearted energy and a great sense of humor. He almost takes it to another level with "my bags are packed and I'm ready to go!" but I'm sure his expressions are just heightened by being at a festival with his friends.

Nadi and I walk to meet up with Luke in the lobby area near where we danced last night. "Good morning!" I say, reaching out to hug Luke, who's standing with his friend Chad.

"Hey, Chad. This is Mimi and her friend Nadi." Luke says. Chad has a hip-hop style to him even though he's in his late 40s. Luckily, we learn right away that Chad is married. Since Nadi is dating someone back at home, it's a more comfortable situation that won't lead to an inadvertent Chad-and-Nadi hook-up.

Just off the resort, Luke, Chad, Nadi and I flag down an open-air jitney car and share it with another couple from the festival who is Bonaire-beach-bound as well. The jitney driver takes us to the festival's chartered yacht, which is heading to the Avila Beach Hotel.

Upon arrival at the Avila Hotel's beach, we find chairs and towels, and we set up our music. Luke, Nadi and I head to the water, while Chad heads to the bar.

turn on #8

It is a pretty overcast day, but we're happy to be visiting a new island and enjoying the relatively quiet beach. "I'm so glad to know you enjoy being in the water," I say to Luke as we jump small waves.

"Well, I was in the Marines. Swimming was one of the ways I stayed fit," he responds.

Nadi, who was also in the military and is a certified swim coach likes Luke even more for me now. "You guys are sooo cute!" she exclaims as she swims away trying to give us alone time.

Luke laughs at Nadi. "She cracks me up," he says. I'm definitely glad they're getting along. Such a stark contrast to her disdain for Leech the first day of the festival – ha!

Luke grabs me around the waist, hoisting me out of the water to jump a wave. His arms stay wrapped around me, and I realize I won't get much swimming in today. This is starting to turn into a semi-romantic beach excursion. I can imagine the few people watching us from the shore thinking 'Get a room!'

"This is really nice, isn't it, Mimi?" Luke comments, still hugging me in the water from behind.

"Yeah, it is," I respond, smiling, yet feeling mildly nervous because I sense Luke's intensity towards me picking up. My prior man experiences tell me to tread lightly.

"So, can you believe I get to celebrate my birthday during the festival?" Luke says.

"Oh, wow, you do? When is it?" I ask.

"It's tomorrow!" Luke says excitedly.

"Oh, nice. We'll have to celebrate!" I say, hoping it doesn't sound too intimate. Then, like a moment out of a movie, after the next wave passes, Luke spins me around for the infamous first kiss. A girl can't ask for much more, really. A big, strong, sexy guy – great personality, Caribbean beach waters dripping off our skin... but I do pull back a little from the kiss because I'm unsure of Luke's angle. I know a lot of guys at the festival are looking for more than a kiss on their seven-day vacay. So, trying not to lead him on, and because I'm really not sure how I feel about him yet, I make the kiss very short. I get the feeling things can progress rather quickly with Luke – physically and emotionally – so I suggest we go grab drinks, lay out on the beach, and listen to Luke's great selection of house music. Thankfully, Luke obliges, and we recess to our beach lounge chairs.

Chad, who had been at the outdoor hotel bar, walks over to our lounge chairs, breaking our veg time. "Hey, do y'all know who that was in our jitney cab earlier?" Seeing our puzzled faces, he answers his own question. "That was Ziggy Marley and his wife! I've been over at the bar having drinks with them; y'all should come!"

turn on #8

Well, so much for a relaxing couple of hours at the beach. I do love music, though, and I'm excited to meet the well-known artist. We gather our things and head to the hotel's beach bar where we get to know Ziggy and his wife. Luke's personality shines through as he talks to the Reggae celebrity, and I can see how likable Luke is. Seeing how fun he is and how many likes we have in common, from dancing, to the beach, to traveling, to meeting new people, I'm thinking maybe there is something here.

Luke, Chad, Nadi and I take the yacht back toward the resort with our newfound reggae music friends, but this time, we're all a little more festive after a few rum runners at the beachside bar. On the jitney bus, I play my personal playlist of Marley music on Luke's portable speakers. We practically turn the ride into a party bus. We're dancing in our seats, waving our hands as the people walking by on the streets stop, look, and dance along with us. It is definitely an unforgettable ride.

We make a quick stop at the souvenir shop just by the resort. Luke reaches out to hold my hand at every chance.

intuition
alarm #6

"You guys look like you've been together for years!" Chad says, teasing us. Chad tells me on the side that he thinks I could be good for his friend. It's so nice of him to say, but it all feels like a bit much for me at this point. I laugh, telling Chad, "Time will tell!" to keep his expectations in check. However, I'm going with the flow because Luke seems like a good guy and might genuinely be into me.

Back at the resort, Luke and I attempt to meet up with our reggae friends for dinner, but they're busy preparing for the nighttime festival concerts. So, Luke and I have a casual dinner together at the buffet before going to the all-white party outside at the pool. Our friends have scattered, somehow thinking we want to be alone. And as much as we encourage them to hang out with us, I guess we're just too affectionate, and maybe it makes our friends miss their significant others back home.

As Luke and I watch the outdoor Usher concert together, he stands behind me with his arms wrapped around my waist. I'm sure that if Chad were nearby, he'd again comment how it looks like Luke and I have been together for years.

While we stand there, comfortably swaying to "You Make Me Wanna," Leech walks by out of the blue. He walks directly in front of us, giving me a death stare since I've pretty much ditched him for Luke. I feel bad, but it's not my fault Leech doesn't' know how to work Wi-Fi, which made it hard to connect with him again. And honestly, I'm relieved because hanging with Luke has been MUCH more enjoyable. Plus, after Leech told me that he's still technically married and doesn't plan to divorce his wife because they have a million dollars' worth of property shared between them, it definitely sounded like more than I want to deal with. After Leech walks past us, I tell Luke why we just received a serious evil eye, and he laughs, holding me tighter. Luke and I continue to dance the night away together, this time watching the reggae concerts and the late-night hip-hop show – another 3:00 a.m. night.

Luke walks me back to my room and makes plans to spend the day together tomorrow in Curacao. He kisses me goodnight – a kiss somewhere between a peck and French. I don't feel sparks from the kiss, though, maybe because I'm not fully allowing myself to embrace Luke yet.

Once in bed, I text Luke, like I did the night before.

Me: Thank you again for a great day. I look forward to helping you continue your birthday celebration in Curacao tomorrow. We'll plan to meet at 10am in the lobby.

Luke: Sure. I'm good with that. I couldn't think of a better way to celebrate my birthday nor could I imagine a more beautiful person to celebrate it with. Goodnight love.

intuition
alarm #6

Wow. The L-word. I know he means it more in a casual sense, but it sends a chill through me. I'm getting the same feeling I had with Vegas: the "too much too soon" feeling. It's only been 24 hours. I try to tell myself that Luke is just being nice and doesn't mean anything serious by the L-word.

CUDDLING IN CURACAO

Big-guy Parker who Nadi introduced me to a couple days ago at blind speed-dating, had offered to show Nadi and I around Curacao since he's been several times before. But, of course, now that I've met Luke and things have escalated with him a bit, I'm unsure whether Parker is alright with me bringing a plus-one along for his chartered flight and tour. I Facebook message Parker, and fortunately, he agrees (though somewhat reluctantly) for Luke to join his Curacao tour.

Luckily, as soon as I introduce Parker and Luke just outside the resort, they realize they both pledged the same fraternity. Though they went to different schools, they have friends in common, including a really good friend, Ralph. Next thing I know, Parker and Luke are giving each other the special fraternity handshake and bonding after only a few minutes.

"Man, this is awesome. A friend of Ralph's is a friend of mine," says Parker. Luke's engaging personality definitely makes for a smoother introduction.

Nadi, Luke, and I walk with Parker to his reserved, full-size van, where the rest of his friends are waiting for us to head to the airport for Curacao. Parker introduces us and we're off for the short flight to the island.

Our first stop in Curacao is a nudist resort – but we're just there for photos. We get out of the van, and Luke and I go for a short walk in the sand. We try to avoid looking at the semi-elderly nude people walking along the shore.

Luke pulls me in for a hug. "You know, Mimi, I really didn't want to come to Curacao. I came here on my honeymoon for my second marriage," he sighs, "but I'm glad we're making new memories here together." He squeezes me tighter as he tells me this.

"Oh, I didn't realize you were married twice..." I comment with surprise while trying not to sound judgmental.

"Yeah, I was. But the first one doesn't really count – it was a rush, and I never should've done it."

Interesting. Well, he is in his late 40s, so being married twice is not out-of-the norm but I wonder if Luke has a pattern of jumping into relationships too soon. Because we met only 48 hours ago, I decide to leave the conversation there. "Well, relationships are not easy, so I get it. It's all good. We'll have fun today," I respond, trying to keep the conversation light.

"Yeah, I'm looking forward to it – this seems like a good group. I'm glad you invited me," he says as he strokes my hair affectionately.

After only a brief walk around the nudist resort, with our clothes intact, we're back in the van, heading to Parker's favorite lunch spot: Hilda's Seafood Restaurant. Luke is in a really good mood, likely due to the serene island views and being on a carefree tour. As we're riding, Luke has his arm around me, as he's caressing my back and holding me close. Nadi, seated in the back of the van, is teasing us with the "oooh, look at you two lovers" eyes. It does feel a bit heavy for me, but Luke is so attractive and so nice that I definitely can't deny his advances.

We arrive at Hilda's restaurant, a rustic seafood spot over-looking the aqua-blue waters of Curacao. The owner knows Parker, and we get a nice big, family-style table on the patio with a great beach view.

Luke is excited for fresh seafood. "I'm going to get the lobster tails, babe," he says happily gazing at his menu. Meanwhile, I'm missing USDA food standards after peeping into the primitive, dark kitchen on the way in. I decide to throw caution to the wind and hope for the best when eating some of Luke's lobster and the huge fresh seafood platter that Parker orders.

turn on #11

During lunch, Luke's likable personality continues to win Parker over, making him root for us despite his attraction towards me. "You know, I really like you two together!" Parker says, biting into a piece of calamari.

Luke keeps the conversation flowing nicely with Parker's friends. "Oh, what do you do?" "And where do you live?" "Where did you grow up?". I always appreciate someone who can carry a conversation – that is a crucial trait I prefer in a man.

As Luke is talking, I happen to look down and discover that his ankle is very swollen. "Oh, my goodness, Luke, was your ankle like that before?" I ask.

"Wow! No, it wasn't. How did this happen?" he asks, rhetorically, with concern in his voice.

"Well don't worry; it happens to me all the time when I travel. I've carried compression socks with me on all my vacations since I was in my 20s. You just need to elevate your feet tonight, and you should be fine." I say.

One of Parker's friends, who is a nurse, hears our exchange from across the table and decides to chime in. "Why don't you let your husband prop his leg on your knee for elevation?" she says.

Nadi, who is sitting next to Luke and me, starts to giggle. Mildly embarrassed, I respond, "Funny, we actually just met at the festival, believe it or not."

The nurse's perplexed looks say it all. "Oh, really? I never would've guessed that. Looks like you two have been together for years," she responds with the rest of the tour group nodding in agreement. In some ways, it's nice to know that we look naturally comfortable together, but I still feel things are moving a bit fast if people are thinking we are married. I try to focus on the positive. After lunch, Luke and I walk out onto the beautiful private beach, where Nadi takes photos of he and I together. Luke loves the "prom pose" where he stands behind me with his arms wrapped around my waist. I continue to go with the flow of our rather intimate moments.

On the flight back to Aruba, Luke shares a little more with me about his military service of 30 years in the Marines. "I went into the service right after high school because I wasn't ready for college. I really didn't try in high school, so I had pretty bad grades."

I chime in, "I see. Well, that makes sense. So, were you in combat with the Marines?" I ask, bracing myself for the answer; I know tough experiences like that can really take a toll on a person's psyche.

"Actually, I was in the human resources department," he responds, to which I breathe a sigh of relief. Luke says he visited many countries with the Marines. Then, when he was in his late 20s, he went to college, graduating cum laude, and later beginning a successful career in advertising. I love an intelligent, successful man, so he is checking the right boxes.

Luke adds, "My only involvement with the military now is helping with burials." *Goodness, that sounds quite morbid*. But he describes it so casually, like there's nothing to it. Luke says the burials are good for supplementing his income. I guess if he's okay with it, and the money is good, what can I say?

"Oh okay, well you have to do what you have to do," I respond.

Back at the resort, it's Luke's actual birthday night, and while I want to be part of the celebration, I definitely don't want to monopolize his birthday – we've been virtually inseparable since we met 48 hours ago. "Hey, so I know we talked about doing sushi tonight for your birthday, but would you rather have dinner with the guys,

intuition
alarm #6

and we can just meet up after?" I ask. He has barely spent any time with the bachelor party group he is here with, and I know they're all having dinner to-gether tonight. Plus, I feel bad that Nadi would be dining alone for the second night in a row if I went for dinner with Luke tonight.

my crazy #11

"I was really looking forward to sushi with you. We can catch up with our friends after," he says. I can't deny him on his birthday, so off to sushi we go. Over sushi, I feel like learning more about Luke's marital situation. "So, how long have you been di-vorced?" I ask while picking up some edamame from our shared appetizer bowl.

"It's been three years, but we just finished a long court battle," he responds with an exhausted tone. "I sued her for part of the house, but unfortunately, I lost my case against her," he says, sounding de-feated.

caution #5

My mind immediately goes to my mini-court bat-tle with my ex-boyfriend, who I had to sue for money I had loaned to him. I can't stand men who take advantage of women, so I'm hoping there's a good reason for Luke's lawsuit against his ex-wife. "That's awful. Was it your house and you had to move out?" I ask for clarity.

"No, I moved in with her when I relocated from D.C. to Florida, but I paid toward the house for seven years, so I felt I was owed some-thing. I just had an awful attorney. It's all online for you to look up," Luke responds.

"Funny you say that. I've been known to look up guys I date on occasion. But you're so transparent I don't see a need to." I say. On the surface, I don't feel Luke was in the right for even bringing the case against his wife, but it's too soon for me to draw any conclusions. Plus, it's his birthday, and we definitely need to lighten the mood.

A couple of Luke's friends who know we're having sushi come over to find us. "Happy birthday, man!" they say as they bring over a bottle of wine for him. They're so thoughtful; he really has a great group.

All our commotion attracts a festival photographer to our area. "Would you guys like to take part in a special photo shoot?" he asks Luke. The photographer explains that he is a beginner and is mainly looking for practice.

Luke, who told me he recently lost 50 pounds, is excited to take photos. "You want to do it, Mimi?" he asks.

How can I say no? Besides, it's just for fun. "Sure, why not. We have time to kill before casino night," I say as we close out our bill. We tell his friends we'll catch them later. What Luke doesn't know is that Leech had asked me to take photos, too, the first night. I thought we were just taking individuals photos, but then he asked for some together. I thought it was a bit much. I'm just hoping Luke doesn't have the same "couples pose" expectations for our photo shoot.

Well so much for that, I say to myself when the photographer encourages us to take photos together.

Despite my look of hesitation, Luke is all in. "Come on, Mimi, it'll be fun!" he says, standing in the empty nightclub waiting for me to stand by his side for the pose the photographer just described. We shoot in several places at the resort, and the poses are very intimate, some with our lips almost touching. I feel like we're compiling photos for an engagement album. I figure the photos will ultimately be fun to look at once developed, but that will be it.

After our unexpectedly sultry photo shoot, we head over to meet up with some of Luke's friends at the casino for the festival event being held there. We order lemon drop shots for Luke's birthday, and we're really having a good time watching some of his friends play blackjack and poker. I excuse myself to step away to the ladies' room for a moment.

On my way, I'm suddenly stopped by a very attractive guy who I have not seen before. He's standing by a group of his friends, in the casino, playing roulette. "Hey there, can I talk to you for a minute?" he asks.

I give him a somewhat perplexed look, unsure of his angle, but I respond, "Yes, what's going on?"

"Are you here with your man?" he asks. Oddly enough, that's a tough question. "Well, no, but I have been hanging out with some-one I met the other day," I respond.

"Oh, yeah, I saw you with that guy over there, the one in the paisley shirt. Are you sure he's even straight?" he asks, prompting laughter from his friends.

While I certainly have reservations about Luke, I definitely know he's straight. I feel the need to defend him. "Well, someone sounds a bit jealous – I actually love his style, personally," I say with confidence.

"Well, I'm Carter, and I think you'll like my style more. Why don't you put your number in my phone so we can stay in contact?" he requests, looking at me with his engaging green eyes. Similar

my crazy #3

to when I met Harper at Mango's while on a date with Vegas, I acknowledge that I have no ties to Luke at this point so, why not? Besides, Carter is attractive, and I don't want to put all my eggs in Luke's basket this early on. Call it FOMO. Casting aside the ounce of guilt inside me, I enter my number into Carter's phone and continue on my way.

Back with Luke and his friends at the poker table, we realize it's time to go catch the 80s band's performance. It's our third night in the row of singing along to our favorite music and dancing until almost 4:00 a.m. I don't know how we do it, but I'm loving it.

Another late-night text:

Me: So glad you had a great birthday. Get a good night's rest...and elevate your ankle! Nte!

RESORT RELAXATION

After several nights of excursions followed by late-night partying, I plan a relaxing day at the resort. I haven't made any particular plans, but once I wake up, Luke invites me to join him in the gym.

Luke: Getting in the shower and late breakfast at Ruinas after workout. Come say hi if you'd like. Will be on treadmill for a while first.

Me: Lol cool thanks for the encouragement. I'll come meet you.

I arrive at the gym to see its great sea views. Luke is running on a treadmill that faces the lightly crashing waves outside. He's sweating and very focused, looking like a true athlete – I'm impressed. "Looking good there," I say, as I wink somewhat flirtatiously. I walk over to a nearby elliptical machine and begin a brief workout. After about 20 minutes, I can tell Luke is really committed to his health – he's looks like the Terminator. He's been running at full speed since I arrived. I guess all those years in the military were not lost on him. And knowing he recently lost 50 pounds, I realize the pressure to keep it off is strong.

Luke keeps his earphones in the entire time at the gym as to not ruin his workout flow. Feeling like he doesn't want to be bothered, I keep to myself and make my rounds in the gym solo. I wave goodbye after about 40 minutes, and Luke is still on the treadmill. I mouth to him, 'I'll see you in a few,' and he suggests that we grab brunch. I was planning to join Nadi for brunch, but with my inability to say no, I oblige Luke instead.

my crazy #5

Back in the room, I tell Nadi I'm going to shower and meet Luke, and she heads off for brunch without me – again. Once I'm out of the shower, I see a text.

Luke: Decided to come eat with the fellas. LOL

Me: Lol I was going to eat with Nadi! But was waiting for you lol.

Luke: I'm sorry babe. Can I make it up to you?

Me: Lol no need to make it up, I'm glad you're spending time with the guys. You should. I can catch up with you later.

Thankfully, I catch Nadi out at the pool bar, and we see a couple cute guys that she knows from back home. It feels nice to flirt a little and be out from under Luke. Nadi and I take pictures with the guys and toast a couple margaritas while I eat brunch. It's too bad that the cuties have significant others back at home; our fun is short-lived.

Luke comes out by the pool, and he and I get seats together to lay out and relax. Nadi is in and out as usual, leaving us mostly by ourselves. Luke and I take in the beautiful sunny afternoon, and the relaxing Aruba trade winds. Luke rests his hand on my thigh – almost like he's marking his territory. Some of his friends stop by to say hi, which is nice, and we're mostly just people-watching together. Since it's so hot, we decide to take a dip in the pool. Once in the water, Luke wraps his arms around me the entire time – again sending warning signals far and wide: She's mine. Luckily, there are a few other couples that are showing strong PDA in the pool, so as before, I go with the flow and don't deny Luke's physical touch.

We spend the evening at concerts together, much like the previous nights. Again, once I'm in bed, I text Luke.

> **Me:** Thanks again for another great day. I'm going to try and be up by 10 to get to the beach by 11. Let me know. Gnte *kisses*

> **Luke:** Ok babe. I will be ready. Good night. You're such a beautiful precious woman. *kisses*

> **Me:** You are amazing all around, grateful to have met you. Look forward to seeing you in the morning. Nte.

I guess the vacation and unlimited time together is escalating our emotions.

BEACH BEHAVIORS

The next morning, we plan to lounge at the resort's beach. Luke texts me at 10:00.

> **Luke:** Ready? Breakfast together? Meet me and Chad?

Well, I sleep in too long and miss Luke's message. Instead, Nadi and I meet up with Luke and the guys on the resort's beach. "Wow, it's packed out here," I say to Nadi as we look for lounge chairs near the water. Walking toward the shore, I see Luke and a couple of his friends. Luke and Chad find two chairs for the four of us to share. It's fine since we want to spend most of our time in the water.

After the chairs get set up, I notice Luke seems a little withdrawn, and oddly, he doesn't want to get in the water. "Luke, is everything okay?" I ask, almost wondering if it's something I did.

"Nah, this morning, over breakfast and since we've been out here, the guys have been teasing me about spending all of my time with you. But I don't care; they're just jealous," he says, sounding like a kid who just had his favorite toy taken away. I have not seen this side of Luke before. I definitely feel like he's over-reacting, and I also feel like his friends have a point. We are spending a lot of time together, and he came on the trip with them. Yesterday, we did try to spend more time with our friends, though, to Luke's credit.

"Well, I'm sure they were just joking with you. I wouldn't worry about it," I say, thinking he'll just let it go.

"They act like I'm the only guy on the trip who met someone. There are other guys who met girls, too," he says still looking and sounding quite frustrated.

"Come on, why don't we get in the water? Some of the guys are already in over there," I say, pointing to his friends, hoping to cheer him up.

"Nah, I don't want to be around them right now," he says as he inserts his earphones, watching concert videos from last night on his phone. He leans back in our shared lounge chair signaling that he is not wanting to do anything else today.

Well ok, this is different. When someone reacts this way, I just give them space because there's nothing I can do. I walk over to catch up with Nadi, who was nearby and heard my exchange with Luke.

"Wow, he's really upset. He's like a totally different person right now," Nadi says.

"Yeah, tell me about it. This is crazy. I don't know if I've ever seen a grown man behave this way – this is not good," I say. I spend most of my time at the beach in the water with Nadi and meeting new people since Luke is completely disconnected. After about an hour, Luke decides to head back to the resort early because he's still frustrated about the guys teasing him for being "attached to me at the hip." I prefer that Luke leaves because I'm not down to coddle a grown man.

I head over to the bar area to listen to the DJ and grab some Caribbean food. "I'll have a pina colada," I say to the bartender, feeling festive and needing to rid myself of Luke's energy.

Hearing my voice, the gentleman next to me at the bar turns around. It's Leech. "Hey, Mimi, long time no see," he says. I'm a little caught off guard. There are thousands of people on the beach, and I forgot all about Leech since Luke started taking up all my time.

"Oh, hey, Rick [his real name]. I haven't seen you in days," I say.

"Yeah, you've been avoiding me. I've seen you around the resort with that guy," he says, rolling his eyes and somewhat teasing me.

"Well, yeah, we've been hanging out. You know I wanted to meet people on this trip, and I'm sure you did, too. We can stay in touch after the festival if nothing else," I say as the bartender passes me my much-needed pina colada. "Well it was good to see you, I'm sure I'll see you around," I say to Leech as I look for Nadi so we can head back inside.

Nadi wants to do a little shopping, so I head back alone. On the way back to the resort, I hear someone call my name. I turn around to see green-eyed Carter and his friend, who are standing and people-watching along the walkway. Carter comes up to give me a hug. "Oh, so you're not with your man, I see."

Goodness, has everyone been watching Luke and me during the festival? "No, he went back to the resort, and he's NOT my man," I say, feeling the need to put distance between Luke and I after his episode on the beach.

"Oh, he's not? You mean you dropped ol' Paisley?" Carter teases, using his nickname for Luke.

"No, we're still hanging out, but trying to give it some space," I respond.

"Oh, so that means you can join us for dinner tonight, then?" Carter asks.

"Well... sure. I can join you all," I respond – especially since I know Luke has dinner plans with the guys.

"Ok, meet us for the Dinner Sail at 6:00. My room number is 610; give me a call."

I meet Carter and his friend for the Sunset Dinner Sail as planned, but I'm turned off by the fact that he keeps talking about how gay "Paisley" is. Instead of talking about himself, all he wants to do is *try* to discredit Luke. And as much as Luke's meltdown earlier turned me off, I'm relieved to get a message from him while at dinner with Carter.

Luke: Missing my baby. Plans after dinner? We hooking up?

Me: Missing you, too. We're definitely hooking up after dinner for the Playboy party tonight. Meet me in the lobby when you're ready.

I leave Carter and head back to my room to change into my new fuchsia Victoria's Secret satin robe. Luke comes to meet me in a navy satin robe, looking as good as ever. His regular mood seems to be back after an evening with the guys, and it's almost like his beach meltdown never happened. Also, seeing Leech and Carter reminded me why I chose to spend so much time with Luke. I give him a hug. "It's good to see you. You look great."

"So do you, Mimi. I love this purple silk robe you're wearing," he says.

Before heading to the party, we decide to check out the photos we had taken. We sit down with the photographer who did our private shoot. "So, here, I put together a package for you two, but you can select any or all of the photos," says the photographer as he pulls out a 20x20 metal-backed canvas-mounted photo of us and an envelope full of glossy 8x10s. I feel like the only thing missing is a cake-tasting because this has serious pre-wedding activity vibes. It's way too awkward to tell this guy we only met a few days prior, so I just play along. Plus, as far as I'm concerned, I only want my solo shots and maybe one of us together for the memories.

"Gosh, Mimi, these are beautiful," Luke says, flipping through the photos. I look at him in disbelief as I realize he's getting caught up and might actually want to purchase several photos of us together. The photos are breathtaking, but I'm afraid Luke is falling for the photographer's sales pitch.

"Yeah, these are really amazing photos, but we only need a couple of them, don't you think?" I say, trying to snap Luke out of the trance he looks like he's under.

"Well, I don't know, Mi. I really can't decide. I think I'm going to get all 10 photos of us together," he says, rubbing his chin like he's in deep thought.

I'm in shock. I look down at the price sheet – all 10 photos cost $200! *Is this guy out of his mind?*

intuition alarm #6

"Mimi, why don't you pick out a couple of solo shots that you like. I'll take care of the payment and meet you outside," he says. I can't believe he's buying so many photos of us together given that we have known each other less than a week, though I am somewhat flattered that he thinks so highly of us that he wants the photos.

"Ok, thanks, babe. I'll be outside," I respond hesitantly as I get up from the table.

Luke walks out with a bag full of photos. I still can't believe he spent $200 on photos mostly of us together. We divide them up and take them back to our rooms. We meet back in the lobby to head to the nearby nightclub. We arrive to find it already packed with people dancing in their Playboy-themed attire, but fortunately we reserved a VIP section for our group. We text our friends to come and join us, and we soon have about eight people sitting around, having drinks and sharing stories from the last several days. We run out of seats, so I sit on Luke's lap to make room and because I am genuinely having a good time with him again.

But (just my luck), after we've there for about an hour, here comes green-eyed Carter, walking way too closely in front of us. He stares at me, making me really uncomfortable, and he keeps walking. I turn around to see that Luke saw Carter's long stare. Luke just rolls his eyes.

"I'm so sorry, Luke, I don't know what's wrong with him. He's crazy," I say.

As I turn back around, Carter is standing over me with his hand extended. "So, you having a good time?" he asks, even though I'm clearly seated on Luke's lap.

Wow, if this isn't just wrong. To diffuse the situation, I simply respond, "Yes, we're good, thank you," and I turn away.

Luckily, Luke takes it all in stride and laughs it off. "Looks like you've got another stalker," he says jokingly.

Nadi, who also saw Carter slide in, messages me from the chair next to me, 'Oh my goodness, the green-eyed bandit is gangsta!'

We all decide to go to the upstairs level of the nightclub for a change of scenery. After being there for about 30 minutes, in walks Carter once again, alone and pacing right by where we're seated. It's insane.

"Gosh, I'm so sorry Luke. I really don't know why he's acting like this. Maybe we should go somewhere else," I say. Luke suggests we head back to the resort's semi-secluded adult pool and lay outside in the cabanas. We leave our friends at the club to relax under the stars outside alone.

"This is nice," I say to Luke as we lay cuddled up together on the cabana bed. I drift off to sleep in Luke's arms as the gentle sound of the sea brings me some much-needed peace from a fun and some-times crazy vacation.

my crazy #5

I wake up about an hour later when the outdoor band starts practicing for the final concert of the trip. Stretching and yawning, I say to Luke, "You want to head inside, babe? I'm getting cold. Plus, I bet Nadi isn't back in the room yet." I am defi-nitely ready for a little alone time with Luke without people walk-ing by.

"Sure. Let's do it," he responds.

We head to my room and Nadi texts that she's still at the club. We get inside the room and lay down on top of the covers. "I've had such a great time with you, Mimi," Luke says, rubbing my face in a way that isn't fully comforting, but I know he means well.

"Yes, you've helped make this vacation very memorable – I'm glad we met. And I look forward to getting to know you more," I say.

"Me too," he responds as he leans in for a long, deep kiss. We're both nervous because we know Nadi could walk in the room at any minute, so our intimacy is short – nothing too passionate, and our clothes stay on. Fortunately, I'm with a perfect gentleman and we keep it PG.

"You know, I'm actually feeling like I should go and join Nadi at the club and closing concerts – one last time to dance the night away before we fly out in the morning," I say.

"You do?" Luke says, stretching then continuing, "I'm actually feeling tired. Plus, I need to get up early tomorrow for our flight and drive four hours home. I think I'm going to head to sleep," he says.

"Well, okay, I think I'll go join Nadi for a little bit," I say as I tighten the belt on my robe and sit up in bed.

"Well, wait, I really don't want you going back out there," Luke says.

I laugh, knowing he's not serious. "Ha, well it's just for a little bit. I'm sure I'll be sleepy soon," I respond, thinking that will end the exchange.

"So, you think I want you to go back to that club, dressed like this and knowing that guy might be there following you around?" Luke says with concern.

"Luke, it's my last night. I just want to have fun. It's only 1:00. I'll be fine," I say convincingly. But then I look at Luke, and he's not budging. Seeing his face, and thinking that it might be best for me to get a good night's rest anyway, I decide to give in. "You know what? I'll just stay in. But I'm not doing this for you. I'm going to stay and get some rest so I'm not exhausted tomorrow for the trip back, too."

Luke gives me a big hug, and minutes later, Nadi comes in for the night, putting to bed any lingering thoughts of going to the club.

DESTINATION: ORLANDO

It's our last morning in Aruba. It's 6:30 a.m. when Luke texts me.

Luke: Good morning baby

Me: Hey babe! Just so you know, I'm still turned on from last night. We are not to be alone anytime soon. Lol

Luke: ;-) *kisses* Call me on your way home.

We talk briefly on the way back home to Orlando, and once we arrive, we exchange 'I'm home safely,' messages. I tell my parents and a couple friends about meeting Luke. I show them our crazy engagement-style photos, to which they respond, "Oh, he's so cute!" and "Wow, this looks serious!" I try to temper their excitement because I have my reservations, but it seems the horse is out of the barn.

Monday morning, Luke and I resume our regular communication, messaging every morning and throughout the workday.

Me: Morning! Did you work out? I am exhausted this morning at work.

Luke: Good morning. Ankles are normal again. Had a great workout. Wanna meet for breakfast this morning at Ruinas after we hit the gym? Meet you at the pool? LOL Miss you baby. *kisses*

Me: Lmao!! Cracking up!! I wish we were back at the Hyatt instead of work lol. Hey, was just about to send you a LinkedIn request. It looks like we have a lot of people in common.

Luke: Cool. Let's connect.

Later that day, I give Luke a call on my way home from work, "So, it looks like Savannah Williams is a friend of yours?" I ask after looking at our shared LinkedIn contacts.

"Yeah, I actually sent Savannah a photo of us as soon as we got back yesterday. She asked how my trip was, and I told her I met this amazing woman. I was shocked when she told me she knows you. She speaks highly of you," Luke says.

"Oh, wow, that is so nice of Savannah. We have mutual friends, so yeah, she doesn't know me THAT well, but I definitely appreciate her telling you that," I say.

"Yes, Savannah is one of my best friends, I talk to her about everything. She's a great person to have in your corner. She's a very prayerful person."

"Yes, I've heard that."

my crazy #6

Knowing Luke and Savannah are close is reassuring. However, I still have reservations about Luke, from the "wedding in Israel" comment to his beachfront meltdown and the excessive photo purchase. At the same time, I feel he's a lot of fun, and he's showing so much interest in me, so I do want to see where things go.

Now that we're back from vacation and reality is setting in, we realize that even though we are less than 20 miles apart, life gets in the way and it's hard to see one another. We plan to meet up again on Sunday – seven days after our return from the trip.

Me: Crazy to think it will take seven days to see each other again and we're just a few miles away but I guess this is real life.

Luke: Yes, I think seeing each other every day at any time of the day on vacation created an unrealistic fantasy… LOL vacation again?

Me: Lol yes, an unrealistic fantasy indeed... but I really enjoyed it and would like to make whatever we establish mirror the adventure we started off with as much as possible. And yes, I'd love to squeeze in another vacation this year, but I've got a lot of time off booked already 😞

Luke: Wow! You vacation a lot huh? I would love to mirror the adventure as well. We had much fun. It was so good getting to know you.

Me: Lol yes gotta live life to the fullest right? Tmw is not promised so I work to enjoy my life. I look forward to having some adventures with you should things go in that direction. I think we learned that we can have a lot of fun together.

Luke: Muah! Yes we can! I'll be your superman.

Later in the day, Luke reaches out:

Luke: I don't have my daughter tonight as I planned and I have to work this conference at the Rosen hotel until 7:30pm. Wanna hook up after? Probably too late since we have to be at work in the morning. Let me know even if we hook up briefly.

Me: Of course! I'll actually be at Eddie V's for dinner nearby so I can come when you free up.

I'm glad we don't have to wait seven days to get together. I pull up to the Rosen Hotel valet, and Luke comes out to meet me. He only has a few moments since he got called into a business dinner a few minutes ago. "Hello sir, can I give you a ride?" I say jokingly to Luke after I let down the window. He jumps in my passenger seat and I drive around the corner to the CVS parking lot.

After I put the car in park, Luke says "Babe I missed you so much," kissing me passionately.

"Me too," I mumble between kisses. Things are getting pretty heated as he kisses my neck and down to my chest. "Oh, my goodness, babe, we have to stop, there are customers around, and I know you have to get back to your dinner," I say.

"Yes, but I'm getting so turned on, I might have to wait a minute," he says looking down at his pants as we laugh in unison. "So, listen Mimi, I want to tell you something. I don't want us to rush into anything physical. I really want us to wait." Luke says with a pretty serious look on his face.

Well, just my luck: first Vegas, and now Luke wants to play coy. "Well, Luke, that is music to my ears. I really try not to 'go there' outside of the confines of a monogamous relationship. But usually, guys want to have fun no matter what, so, I'm happy to hear you say you want us to wait. Is it that you want to wait for marriage for religious reasons?" I ask, for clarity.

Laughing, Luke responds, "No, no, not at all. It's not like that. I just want it to be special, you know?" he says, holding my hand and looking at me rather innocently.

"Sure, I understand, I want that too. I definitely want to wait," I say. We kiss a little bit longer before I drive Luke back around to the hotel valet and we say goodbye. "So, maybe we can catch up tomorrow? I'll be at Rocco's Tacos for happy hour," I say after he closes the door.

"Yes, I want to try and come by," he says as he waves goodbye.

It's happy hour at Rocco's Tacos, and some of our mutual friends are here: Ray from the festival and his wife Felicia, and other friends of ours, Alex and Renee. I text Luke, trying to get him to Rocco's.

Me: Ray and Alex say hi! They won't stop talking about you though and how great you are. You should pay these people, they're your biggest advocates lol.

Luke: Wow! I'm not surprised, and that's not arrogance. I am genuinely a good guy. I am a reflection of God's grace *kisses*

By the time Luke arrives, Ray, Alex and their wives have left so Luke and I go across the street to Vines for a drink on the patio. We both fall asleep in no time, still likely exhausted from the trip last week. "This is crazy. How did we hang out so late every night on the trip and now we can't stay up past 9:00?" I say as we laugh. We kiss goodnight and agree to meet up again on Sunday evening.

Me: Morning babe. Enjoy church service and your workout.

Luke: Good morning. Off to praise God. See you soon.

That evening, as planned, I pull up to Luke's apartment for the first time. It's really nice; it's bright and modern on the outside. He has lived here for three years, since his divorce. "Hey babe," I say as I get out of the car and give Luke a hug.

"Hey, Mimi. I'm glad you made it over," he says, squeezing me tightly. We begin to walk toward the four-story apartment building which has several sections. "Why don't I give you a quick tour of the grounds, and then we can go grab a bite to eat?" he says.

"That sounds good to me!" I respond. Luke walks me around the beautiful amenities of his apartment, showing me the gym, the movie room, the fire pit and the pool. I almost feel like he wants his neighbors to see him walking with a girl, though he doesn't seem to know anyone in the complex. After the quick tour, we take the elevator upstairs to his car and drive about 10 minutes to Capital Grille for dinner.

Walking up to the restaurant, Luke initiates holding hands. I'm not big on hand-holding, but as always, I don't deny his affection.

"Table for two?" the hostess asks before leading us to a high-top table by the opened patio doors.

"So, busy day?" I ask Luke as we sit down, and the waiter fills our water glasses.

"Yeah, it was. I took my daughter to church, dropped her back off at her mother's house, and then worked out before you came over," Luke says.

"Oh okay, another pretty full day for you," I say, taking a sip of water. I talk about my day with my parents for their anniversary, but because he no longer has his parents, I keep the conversation brief. He had mentioned how hard it is hearing other people talk about their parents.

"May I take your drink order?" the waiter asks, standing next to us in his starched white coat. Luke hands me the wine list, and I ask the waiter to give us a moment. He steps away. "Luke, you know I'm not going to be able to come back to your place after this. If I have a drink, I might be tempted to do some things that we said we wouldn't," I say.

"Waiter, we need drinks!" Luke jokes. He does have a great sense of humor. "Well, you know I want you to come over and see my place – we can just watch a movie. You don't have to stay long, but I do want to have some alone time with you finally," he says.

"I agree, I want that, too," I say. Luke orders us a bottle of Pinot Noir to share. I order a salmon salad, and he orders a steak.

Drinking our wine, I mention, "So, I don't think I know how your marriage ended," trying to understand how this guy who is so well-loved by his friends could have had a marriage end in such a nasty court battle.

"You know, she and I don't even speak anymore. When we're at our daughter's basketball games – like yesterday – my ex, and especially her mom, won't even look my way," he says.

Yikes, I'm thinking to myself. *It's bad enough that he sued her for part of the house but knowing that she doesn't speak to him?*

It definitely sounds like there is bad blood. "That's so unfortunate, Luke, especially with your daughter seeing this. How did it get so bad?" I ask.

"Well, she stopped having sex with me years ago. I was celibate for three years of our marriage; she wouldn't sleep with me. And finally, one day, I found a dildo in the house and I hit the roof. It didn't make any sense to me that she didn't want to be with me but wanted to use a toy instead," he says.

"Wow, wow, wow, Luke, that is really crazy," I say, taking in two sips of wine to swallow the discomfort of his story. "So, what do you think the root cause was?"

"Well, I really didn't like that she didn't come to church with me and our daughter. I mean, what kind of woman will let their child go to church and not go with them?" he asks somewhat rhetorically.

"Well, Luke, you know that I do not attend church, but at the same time, I do believe in exposing a child to faith, so I understand where you are coming from," I say, "but you know I'm not going with you to church, so maybe we're better off as friends given that that was a deal-breaker for you with your wife." I'm somewhat sad that I am about to lose him over our differences in our beliefs.

"Well, no, it's different with you. You're not the mother of my child. You don't have an obligation to go with me like she did," he says.

"But don't you want a woman who is going to be there with you in the pew, someone who will read the Bible with you?" I ask.

"Well, I am trying to read the bible more and get deeper in my faith," he says, "but at the same time, I can respect where you are, and I really just feel like we'll be okay." He stands up and kisses me passionately while I'm still seated on the bar stool. Between the wine, his kiss, and the dizzying conversation, I'm just in a lull, so when he suggests I come back to his apartment, I oblige hoping he will stick to his "let's wait" promise.

We leave Capital Grille and head back to Luke's apartment. Walking in, even with the lights low, I can see it is very clean and decorated very nicely. He gives me a full tour, and I feel right at home, which is a good feeling.

We sit down on the couch, and he turns on the TV. I have no clue what's on because in no time, we're fully making out, his hands under my flowy cotton blue dress and my arms wrapped around his head as I straddle him.

"Luke, Luke, we have to stop... right?" I ask as he kisses me to quiet my caution. We keep kissing, and Luke picks me up and takes me into the bedroom. He lays me down and pulls down my thong. I try to stop him, but before I know it, his face is buried between my legs, and it takes everything in me to say, "Luke, *gasp* we're supposed to wait," though I don't really want him to stop.

We agree to stop, and Luke just holds me. It always feels nice *physically* in his arms because he is such a tall guy, but I feel a little unsettled at the same time. All the things that Luke has said play back in my head, and tonight's revelations about his ex-wife who hates him and didn't sleep with him for years is definitely alarming. But I have several ex-boyfriends who don't speak to me either, and we don't have anything near a child, house or marriage between us, so I can only imagine how my exes would treat me if we had real issues to disagree over. I try to leave Luke's marital past in the past and hope that my future with him will be brighter.

I head home after about an hour at Luke's place. We agree that our next meet-up will be Friday and that we *might* include an overnight stay.

BEDROOM BEHAVIORS

It's another busy week for Luke and for me, but we stay connected via text as usual.

Luke: We need sleep.

Me: Lmao, right, we shouldn't be sleeping together for a few reasons and yes, getting adequate sleep is one of them. But we need this Friday night sleepover so we can sleep in. Then we can go for a jog Saturday.

Luke: That would be fun. Seriously.

Me: But only if you promise to keep your clothes on for the sleepover.

Luke: No tasting either?

Me: Ha. I was going to say no more tasting! That was NOT supposed to happen the other night! Totally caught me off guard, it was dark, and I couldn't stop you...

Luke: I didn't want to, but you provoked me, and I couldn't control myself. That's my story and I'm sticking to it.

Me: You see how emotional I get with the level of intimacy we had Sunday night? We can't go there again... Want to make decisions with my mind, not my body or my heart. And ha, I totally didn't provoke you!

Luke: If you weren't so beautiful, it would be easy. Your mom's fault for producing a beautiful intelligent sexy daughter.

Me: I thought we were going to your place to watch a movie, not make one! Aww but thank you babe for the compliments.

Later in the week...

Luke: Not sure if your ears were burning but had a conversation with a client about you. He's an avid

Christian – Seventh-day Adventist and recommended readings that he felt will help with your quest for answers. And yes, I plan to read them.

Me: Lol, I'll have to find some other readings on the case for non-belief ;-)

Luke: Cool. It's only a quest for understanding and answers not debate. We both believe what we believe but our minds are open enough to receive all opinions and observations for deeper understanding and clarity. ☺

Me: 100% babe… 100%. ☺

Luke: I'm intrigued, truly.

Me: I know you are babe, you're passionate about everything you do. Love your heart. We are more alike than we are different.

Luke: I just want love, peace and harmony ☺

Me: Exactly… me too. And I think that's why we get along so well, we're both good-hearted people. When you connect to a pure soul, there's nothing better. And I think that's why ppl we're so excited about us bc at least in my experiences it seems the wolves in sheep's clothing latch on to us and take advantage… Too often good people miss connecting with good people.

Luke: Absolutely but there always seem to be something in question that causes one to hesitate and question the purpose/reason for the connection or compatibility. Which is why I keep reaching the conclusion that our thoughts and actions should be free, open, slow and deliberate. Do you agree that we should keep dating other people in the process? Although, I must share with you I requested that my Match profile be canceled and deleted yesterday because it is not producing the results I want and feel it has been a waste of time and resources.

Me: Lol well of course I'm happy you deleted your Match profile… even though it had nothing to do with me 😊 And I agree that we should continue dating other ppl (though I'm not intimate with anyone else) bc our situation is so new.

intuition alarm #6

Luke: Mimi, I feel a very positive soothing vibe from you and could easily just move hastily to making you my lifelong partner. However, my baggage and prior experiences are causing me to be wiser and more cautious. You are a good woman. Although I'm sure there is more to learn about you. I'm thinking of kissing you right now. LOL

Me: Lol aww you're the best babe. My heart is pure and I feel a very strong positive energy from you as well. I think we have great potential bc we get along well, we respect one another, we enjoy doing the same things and we have good hearts. I'd love for us to work but yes, we will proceed slowly and with caution.

Luke: *kisses*'

A few days after our steamy after-dinner rendezvous, I run into Luke's and my mutual friend, Savannah. Savannah is attending my organization's charity fundraiser at Kres restaurant downtown. "So, I hear you met Luke in Aruba?" says Savannah in her Southern accent, smiling and half-teasing me.

"Yes, he and I have so many mutual friends. It's crazy that we didn't meet earlier," I respond, facing Savannah and sipping a glass of Cabernet.

Savannah, who has been married for over 30 years and is well-respected in the community, couldn't have better things to say about Luke. "Well, Luke is like a little brother to me. He's such a good guy. We talk all the time."

Shaking my head, I acknowledge what she is telling me. "Yes, Luke told me how close the two of you are. I have to say, I have only heard great things about Luke, which is really nice," I respond. Savannah's glowing remarks only make me cast my doubts about Luke aside.

The next morning, Friday, we text each other.

Luke: Good morning Mimi.

Me: Good morning. Guess I should wake up since I need to throw clothes in a bag and get ready for the weekend at your place.

Luke: Yes. Pack and get ready to be at your second home.

Me: Lol lol, may you always feel that way.

Luke: I'm feeling really good about you. I pray that you're everything I am perceiving you are. I've always wanted a woman who is professional, ambitious, goal oriented, God-fearing, beautiful, sexy, down to earth, well-groomed and dressed, clean and organized, feminine, healthy and fit and allows a man to assume his role in all aspects.

Me: Haaaa!! Yes you deserve all of that and you can only find that in one person… ME! ;-)

Luke: Awwww, thanks babe. That's my prayer. We'll see.

Me: Lol… but seriously, I hope to make you happy.

Luke: So, Saturday, I have to go to my daughter's basketball game at 11am after you and I go for our morning run, but you can relax at my place, have a good lunch, sleep and watch TV until I return.

Me: Sounds like heaven, thanks babe.

Luke: Cool huh?

Me: That you trust me that much to be in your place without you? Yes.

Luke: Absolutely. You're top-shelf quality. Just wish we could go grocery shopping so you have all that you're accustomed to eating or snacking on perhaps something to cook for lunch.

Me: Aww thank you babe! Glad you recognize quality. Of course, the feeling is totally mutual. If we come back from jogging early enough, I can grab sushi or something like that from Publix.

Luke: Cool. I want you to cook and put some love in the food. LOL

Me: Ohhh you want me to cook tmw afternoon. That's fine, if we have time after jogging, we can grocery shop.

Luke: Then again, I don't know. You might put some mojo in the food and I'll be tied up walking down the aisle.

Me: Only aisle we need to go down is the one at Publix. And the only carats I need are orange.

Luke: You gone cook in lingerie? Another Playboy night like in Aruba?

Me: Haaaa!! Right, might as well!

Luke: Oh, I have to participate in a burial on Sunday morning, so you can sleep in then, too.

Me: Convenient. Then I should have omelets ready by the time you get back ;-)

Luke: You're a real MVP.

It's our first weekend together, and I'm nervous, mostly because I know how hard it will be to keep our commitment "to wait," but I'm confident we can behave.

I arrive at Luke's apartment after a full workday followed by a banquet. He had a business dinner after work, so we are both pretty tired. Plus, we have plans to get up at 6:00 to head to the jogging trail, so we shower and get in bed for our first night together.

"I like that negligee, Mimi," Luke says as I climb under the blanket with him in his big and very comfortable king-sized bed. We pretty much pick up where we left off on Sunday when I stopped by "to watch a movie" after dinner. In the middle of a steamy make-out session, Luke tries to gently pull off my thong when I stop him.

"What are you doing babe? You know we're supposed to wait," I say, moaning, knowing I really don't want to wait anymore. Luke doesn't respond and just proceeds to pull off my thong. I'm not sure why I thought this would go any differently. I know I shouldn't give in, but I can't help myself, and the passion overcomes me. At least we had the STD conversation before my willpower collapsed.

Luke certainly doesn't disappoint. All the stamina he has from his intense workouts, coupled with his natural strength, make for a good time. Luke does most of the work delivering several rounds of pleasure using every tool in his arsenal. After about 45 minutes of action in his massive bed, we pass out curled up next to one another. I feel like we're officially connected now – it has been some time for me, and while I still have reservations, I think we might be able to make this work.

Luke kisses me passionately, as he holds me. He seems to have zero regrets about us breaking our promise. And I'm thinking it was just a matter of time, so I'm comfortable that we took this step in our relationship. He reaches over for his sleep apnea mask, ending all intimacy, and we drift off to sleep to the sound of his machine.

Luke wakes me up at 5:30 a.m. and climbs on top of me, ready to go at it again. I'm 10 years younger than he is, and I should be ready, too, but I've never been one for morning *activity*. Not to disappoint him, though, and because he is doing 90% of the work, I moan and move in the right directions, so I can hopefully get a little more sleep after we're done. He is so caring, rubbing my face, kissing me with emotion. I'm grateful he is talented in the bedroom. However, he is not the smallest guy "down there," so I'm not looking forward to going for a run after all of this activity.

"Mimi, it's 6:00. We had better get going so we're not out in the sun too long. Plus, remember I have my daughter's basketball game at 11:00. and we have to get you back here before then," he says.

Well, so much for getting any more sleep. I had a feeling that, with his military ways, reneging on the morning run was not an option.

turn on #10

Luke jumps out of bed, showers, and proceeds to pack healthy snacks, including yogurt, bananas and granola bars, and plenty of water for our run. With his recent weight loss, he definitely takes his health seriously, and I can appreciate that. He shows me a salad in the fridge that he made for later, but he also has a steak in the freezer that he wants me to prepare – works for me. I'm fairly healthy but do like to cheat, so I feel like we are aligned in our eating habits.

We go out to Luke's truck, and being the gentleman that he is, he opens the door for me. "Oh, let me move that out of your way," he says as he moves his two Bibles and Christian music CDs from the passenger seat to the middle console. Just in case we needed a gentle reminder to repent from last night's transgressions, I suppose. "Hmm, I guess this is a sign," I say jokingly.

"Yeah, you need to read it," Luke says teasing me as we laugh.

We get out of the car at West Orange Trail. Luke is in focus mode for his 10-mile run. He downs a banana like a gorilla and hydrates himself before lacing up his sneakers. He checks in on Facebook. "I have to tell my virtual running group I'm here," he says as I see a look of competition and determination come over his face.

I see he takes running very, very seriously. I suppose I shouldn't be surprised after seeing "the Terminator" on the treadmill when we were in Aruba.

"So, it'll probably take me about an hour before you see me heading back towards you, okay?" he asks, making sure I'm okay since he's going to start out jogging with me and then speed up to get his desired distance.

"Yes, I'll be fine, I'm used to power walking out here alone," I say since I was always last with my job's running group.

We get going and Luke is a beast on the trails. I couldn't keep up with him if I tried. Luke speeds off and circles back for me at after his long run and jogs slowly again with me. It's a beautiful sunny Florida day, and you can feel the summer heat and humidity are about to pick up, so we head back to the car after he completes his 10 miles.

"This was fun, Luke. I'm glad we came out today," I say, feeling accomplished.

turn on #8

I do like that the one activity he is really passionate about is something we can do together. If he loved golf, I might join him occasionally, but power walking is something I can do often. And though I'm nowhere near as committed as he is, I'm glad that he'll be a motivator for me to walk more often, which I need to do.

Back at Luke's apartment, we take showers, and he heads to his daughter's basketball game. I agree to have a late breakfast ready for him when he returns: steak and eggs.

Finally seeing his apartment in the light of day, I walk around and can really appreciate how nice it is. He has excellent taste in furniture, which he told me he had imported. And then I notice there are several places throughout his apartment that reflect his deep religious beliefs. On the wall, he has a 12"x5" statue of Jesus. In his bathroom, he has water from his baptism in the Sea of Galilee and sand from Israel. A bible verse is quoted on the guest bathroom wall. There is no doubt that Luke is fully immersed in his faith.

caution #6

Also, in his bathroom, I see that stacked up on shelves next to his bathtub are bottles upon bottles of hydrogen peroxide and baby oil. Luke had shared previously that he likes to take baths with both products – definitely a new one for me, but I can appreciate a man who is so into cleanliness. Like everything else with Luke, I can see he is 'religious' about his cleansing routine, considering that he has more hydrogen peroxide bottles than the local CVS pharmacy.

After Luke returns from basketball and gets settled on the couch, he demolishes the meal I cooked. "Mimi, this is great. Thank you," he says, cutting into the last piece of steak.

"Oh, good. I'm glad you enjoyed it. How was basketball?" I ask.

"Oh, Trinity was great out there. She scored the most points! I'm so proud of her," he says, glowingly.

"That's awesome. I'm sure she was glad you were there," I respond.

"Yeah, I try not to miss a game. Even her grandparents came out today," he says with slight sarcasm.

"Oh, that's nice. So, you got to see them?" I ask.

"Yeah, but they just act like I'm not there. Ever since the court case, they don't speak to me," Luke says. I'm envisioning now, that if things escalate with Luke, I'd be thrown into the middle of his family drama. I don't mind as much if I can support someone's view, but unfortunately, I'm not sure I support Luke suing his ex for a portion of the house she initially bought. But we're far from me ever meeting his kids, his ex or her family, so I let it go.

Luke suggests we go get mani/pedis, and I'm all in. It's a first for me to have a guy treat me, and he is like a celebrity at the nail salon, apparently, since he goes regularly.

On our way back to his apartment, one of Luke's brothers, who lives in Baltimore, calls. He is in town at the theme parks with his girlfriend. "Hey man... Oh, so y'all want to come by the house later?... Ok cool. And maybe we can hit a club or something?... Ok, see y'all around 8:00," Luke says before he hangs up. He had mentioned earlier that one of his brothers was in town, but I didn't realize I was going to get to meet him. "So, Mimi, does that work for you? We can hang out with my brother and his girlfriend tonight?" Luke asks.

"Sure, I'm open," I say.

"Well, let's stop by Publix and get some food. Maybe you can make your favorite meal? I have some seafood in the fridge that we could use," Luke suggests. I'm flattered Luke is taking us seriously enough that he wants me to meet his brother, so I'm happy to make dinner. And lucky for him, I like impromptu get-togethers and making plans on the fly.

"Ok, sounds good. Let's go by Publix so I can get a few things," I respond.

Back at Luke's apartment, after getting a few groceries, I pour a glass of wine and get back in the kitchen. I haven't cooked twice in one day in years. At least, I do enjoy cooking, and it helps a lot that Luke has a great kitchen where I feel comfortable.

It takes longer than I realize to make the pasta dish with seafood and two sauces, so I rush to shower and get dressed before his brother and girlfriend arrive. "Mimi, can you get the door?" Luke yells from his bedroom; he isn't dressed yet.

Well, thank goodness I'm a people person now that I will be his brother's greeter. "Sure, I'll get it," I say as I walk to open the door.

"Hi! Welcome!" I say, somewhat jokingly as I open the door. I'm feeling a bit odd that I'm appearing like the "lady of the house."

Meanwhile, his brother knows I've only known Luke for less than a month. "Oh, you must be Mimi," Luke's brother says, smiling.

"Yes, and you must be Tim," I say, laughing at the slight awkwardness of it all. I shake his girlfriend's hand as they walk in and settle around the kitchen bar stools. I can tell there is nothing stuffy about this couple at all; his brother especially seems very cool and laid back.

"So, are you guys hungry?" I ask.

"Well, we actually ate before we came, but seeing as you went through so much trouble, I'll have a small plate," Tim says.

"Ok, cool," I say as I turn to prepare a bowl of pasta for his brother with garlic bread.

"Hey, man, y'all made it!" says Luke as he emerges from his bedroom, dressed to go out to the club. I had learned that some of my friends are going to Mango's tonight, so we decide we will join them later and show Tim and his girlfriend a good time.

Luke and Tim hug, and I can see a slight resemblance between them. Tim is very outgoing and seems a lot like Luke. His girlfriend is pretty quiet as she just sits, still wearing her hat and not fully engaging.

"So, Luke says y'all just met at the Aruba music festival recently?" Tim says to me almost rhetorically.

"Yeah, it's kind of crazy that we had to meet on a Caribbean island when we live in the same city and have so many friends in common," I respond.

"Well, that's really cool, though. So y'all had a good time?" Tim asks.

"Yeah, it was great. If you love music, it's a must in my opinion," I respond.

Luke pulls out the professional pictures he bought at the festival. "Hey, man, check out these photos I got." Most of the 40 or so photos are of Luke – which, to me, is a bit much – but then when Tim sees our couple's photos, you can tell he thinks it's odd that we have such intimate poses, but he tries to play along,

"Oh, wow, these are nice photos, man," Tim says, continuing to flip through. I try to put the blame for our couples-photos on the photographer and lessen the pressure on Luke from being teased.

"I know my little brother. This is just like him. Did he tell you about his first marriage?" Tim asks.

"Well… not exactly," I respond, looking at Luke for him to approve this exchange. Surprisingly, Luke doesn't stop his brother as he starts telling the first marriage story from his perspective.

caution #7

"Well, he only knew this girl for a few months, and next thing I know, he's telling me he's moving from D.C. to St. Louis to be with her. A few months later, he has me flying over to be in this elaborate wedding. She must've spent – what? – $100K on that wedding. I remember her having a closet full of furs and designer purses. She drove expensive cars, but at the same time, her fridge was empty, and she didn't always pay her bills. It just didn't make sense. I saw a lot of red flags and tried to talk Luke out of it, but when he sets his mind to something, he's like a bull. You just can't change his direction," Tim says while Luke shakes his head.

I'm surprised Luke is okay with Tim telling me all of this because it definitely doesn't paint Luke in a favorable light, but I guess Luke figures I'd find out eventually.

Luke adds his perspective. "She was a very successful financial advisor, and we were only married for a few months before I realized she was crazy, and I got out. She eventually ended up in jail on corruption charges."

Wow. He sure knows how to pick 'em. My red flags are going up even more now. Luke's rush to judgment in marrying his first wife reminds me how quickly things with he and I are developing. And the story of him moving into her house reminds me of how he moved into his second wife's house. When relocating cities, it makes sense to move into your girlfriend's house, but at the same time, it doesn't sound like Luke ever took the lead financially in his relationships – and I know that is important to me. I don't want to be with someone who tries to take advantage of me. I didn't get that impression from Luke in our brief dating experience – he has picked up every bill and has been a perfect gentleman. But I do realize he is almost 50 and doesn't own any property of his own. I can only hope at this point that he is financially stable. He seems to have a successful career in advertising now, so I don't believe money will be an issue.

"Well, I was really young back then. When I married her, I was in my early 30s," he says, trying to convince me that he is no longer such a bad judge of character. I just reflect on the good things we have between us and hope that Luke has changed.

We head to Mango's and meet my friends Gisela, Leila and Rachel. It's their first-time meeting Luke, and they are so excited for me. "Oh, wow, Mimi, he's so cute. I'm so happy for you!" says Rachel. They always want me to settle down and even though I don't feel fully settled yet, I try to get comfortable in this new relationship space.

Luke and I go upstairs to the dance room where we see a group of people celebrating a birthday. It turns out we know some of the guests. "Oh, Luke, look – there's Savannah's sister. Do you want to go say hi?" I ask.

"Yeah, I see her and some of the other women. They're friends with my ex-wife. They're so fake and pretentious. Let's go over here instead," he says, ushering me away from the birthday group.

Well, this is awkward. I have an ex in town who I don't enjoy seeing, so part of me understands Luke's reservations with seeing his ex-wife's friends, but Orlando is so small. *Will I always have his ex-wife's life in my shadow?*

Savannah's sister eventually comes up to us to say hello – perhaps a fact-finding mission on her part. It's quick and painless, though, and we proceed to hang out with his brother on what is pretty much a low-key night. Luke seems turned off by the presence of his ex-wife's friends and is nowhere near as lighthearted and fun as he was in Aruba when we were dancing the night away at the clubs. It definitely seems like it's really hard for him to shake it when he gets upset about something.

Back at the apartment, his brother and girlfriend say goodbye. Luke and I are exhausted from a long day. We get in bed and fall asleep. Tonight is nowhere near as steamy as the night before. In the morning, Luke gets up early because he has a long drive to conduct a military burial. He wakes me up and gets fully dressed in his military attire. He kisses me goodbye. "Make yourself comfortable, Mimi. I should be back around noon, and maybe we can go to the pool," he says. I wonder how people can do funerals and not have it affect them emotionally, but Luke seems to like the money, and he doesn't complain. I turn on the TV in his big comfy bed and try not to over-think "us." I turn on Oprah's Super Soul Sunday and veg out.

turn on #10

Luke returns and gets into bed with me. We decide to snack on nachos and cheese (two of my secret vices: eating nachos and eating in bed – so glad we share this in common). We proceed to have a relaxing Sunday together. After a few hours of watching Bill Maher episodes and an old Michael Moore movie, Luke says, "Why don't we go out to the pool? It's such a nice day." I agree, and I love that he enjoys pool time.

turn on #8

We pack-up our nachos to go, along with a few other snacks, and head to the pool. I turn Luke on to a relaxing Pandora music channel, and we stretch out and fall asleep by the pool. We did have a long day on Saturday, so it's no wonder we're tired. Later, we order Thai food takeout, and I join Luke on his couch for his favorite pastime: watching tennis. He's obsessed with tennis and has to watch every set. I realize that if we are going to work out as a couple, I'll have to occupy myself while he binges on tennis – I just can't watch it. Luke starts to get a little frisky on the couch, and we take the action to the bedroom, where we pass out afterward. Luke totally misses the end of the match.

It's Monday morning, and we both have to get ready for work. Luke turns on the bedroom TV to CNN at 6:00 and gets in the shower. Though I have time to sleep in, with his gigantic TV blaring, I don't have a chance of falling back to sleep. This will be yet another adjustment for me. He kisses me goodbye, and I let myself out of his apartment about an hour later, placing his apartment key under the mat.

Me: Morning again ;-) Just getting settled in at work, reflecting on the weekend and grateful for all you did for me. I really had a great time from the morning run, to mani/pedis, to Mango's, to dinner with your bro, to pool time. I hope you enjoyed the wknd as well. Have a great day!

Luke: Thank you sweetie. The feeling is mutual. Awesome weekend. Have a great day!

TO THE LIMIT

The work week flies by. Luke and I are not able to sync schedules and get together, but we have planned to spend the weekend together again. After Friday night dinner with my co-workers, I get to Luke's place just as he's heading to bed. He's intent on getting up at 5:00 a.m. to go running because he didn't work out all week. We have a quick round of intimacy before falling asleep.

The next morning, we hit the trail together again. He runs like a maniac, trying to make up for the lack of calories burned during the week. I can tell he's frustrated with himself that he didn't work out. Afterward, we run errands and return to his apartment for a quiet Saturday night in. It almost seems we have established a routine – we're like a couple that has been together for years. I feel somewhat comfortable, but something inside me is still unsettled.

Sunday morning, Luke gets up early to go to Sunday service. He kisses me goodbye. "Babe, I should be back by 11:00," he says. After he leaves, I have time to think about us and how things are progressing. I walk around his apartment and find myself aimlessly dusting surfaces and window sills while thinking. Of the myriad of question marks I have in my head about Luke, the most significant one is whether our relationship can withstand our differences in faith. My friend Joy, who is Christian, has been happily married to her agnostic husband for over 20 years. I tell myself that I can make this work, though I'm not sure I'm fully believing it on the inside.

When Luke returns from church, he climbs into bed with me, and as sacrilegious as it seems, we have sex. Afterward, Luke decides he wants to take a bath – with peroxide and baby oil because that's his thing. He invites me to join him, and we keep it PG in the tub before toweling off and retiring to the patio to relax. We wanted to drive out to the beach today, but we aren't up to it, so instead Luke gets some outdoor cleaning done.

He turns on my relaxing Pandora station (which he now loves). He doesn't want my help cleaning, so instead, I stretch out on the patio to keep him company. "So, tell me more about your son. He's in college now, right?" I ask while Luke is wiping down the patio windows outside.

"Yeah, and he's doing extremely well. I'm so proud of him," he says.

"Oh, that's great. I'm happy to hear that. Well, how about his mother, your ex-girlfriend – where is she?"

"She's in Baltimore with her new husband."

"Oh, I see. So, did you get to see your son a lot while he was growing up since she lived so far away?"

"Well, I didn't even know about him at first. She was my girlfriend while we were in the military in Arkansas. She told me she was on the pill, and when she got pregnant, she didn't tell me. She left camp abruptly, and I didn't know why until months later when she called me when she back at home with her parents in Texas. I flew down to see her and my son, and her family shunned me. It turns out she told them that I had raped her."

Wow. As if the story of the first wife wasn't bad enough, this one is much worse. "That is awful, Luke. How did you handle that?" I ask, sadly.

"Well, she eventually told her parents that she made up the rape story. I then talked her family into letting her move back to the base in Arkansas with me. But once she came with me, I realized it was just too much. And then I did something I really shouldn't have, I told her that she would come to my next military location with me but, instead, I flew out of state without her and my son and didn't tell them I was leaving."

"Oh, my goodness, that is awful! How could you leave your son?" I ask, feeling like I'm seeing a whole other darker side of Luke.

intuition
alarm #7

"I was just really young, and I didn't know how to handle things. Leaving my son and his mom is one of my biggest regrets in life," Luke says.

I'm watching Luke scrub his windows and I'm just thinking how much I really don't know him. I feel pretty queasy. I'm not sure how much more I can take. I feel the need to change the subject. "So, how was church this morning?" I ask, wondering if he's feeling any apprehension that I was not there with him.

"Oh, it was good. The Pastor talked about forgiveness. I feel like it was a message for me to reach out to my ex and her fiancé, but that will take a lot of time. I have to focus on my own heart before I can involve her in the equation of reconciliation," he says, squeezing out his sponge into the bucket of water.

"Wow. Yeah, I'm sure it will take a lot, but at least you're starting down the right path," I respond automatically, though my reservations about Luke are very much swirling in my head.

There's something about my chemistry with Luke today that is slightly off. The passion and excitement from the trip and even from our first weekend together are weakened, and with each passing story – the crazy convict first ex-wife, the second ex-wife who he lost a court battle to, and now hearing that his son's mother accused him of rape before saying she made it up – it's all just becoming a bit too much. I know I shouldn't have let things get physical before I found out more about Luke, but now I don't want to stay with him just because of the pressure from our friends and from him to make things work. "Luke, was there a part of you that wanted me to be in church with you today? Do you think you'll ever be okay with kissing me goodbye and heading to church, leaving me in bed?" I ask, feeling like I already know the answer.

"Well, maybe you'll change your mind and come with me. It's only a couple hours, and the Pastor is really great," he says.

I can't explain it, but sitting here on his patio, reflecting on where we are, I just feel like we have come to a crossroads much sooner than I ever would've imagined. "Luke, I'm really wondering if we would be better off as friends," I say, letting the words slip out then feeling immediately nervous about his reaction. He might feel like this is coming out of left field, though it has been brewing for me pretty much since we met.

"Really?" Luke asks. "Why do you think that?"

"Well, I see your passion for your faith. It's evident all over your apartment with the Jesus statue, the baptismal water, the two Bibles in your car. I just feel like I'm not allowing you to be fully you and that you'd be better served by a woman who is happily by your side every Sunday and helping you grow into the strong Christian man you want to be. There are so many women out there who would love that, and I just think it would be best for you. When I was deeply religious, I would've done anything for a man like you. I know how great a relationship can be when you are aligned on faith."

"Mimi, I'm happy with what we have. Let's just see where things go, okay?" Luke says.

Usually, I'm weak in these circumstances, but feeling the weight of everything I now know about Luke, I stand my ground. "Listen, I still want us to be friends, but I just don't feel like I'm the right girl for you. I really have strong feelings for you, but I'm trying to think logically about this," I say, sounding stronger than I feel.

"Well, Mimi, if that's your choice, there's nothing I can do. Just know I don't want things to go this way," he says.

"I know, Luke, I know," I say as I stand up to give him a hug. "Maybe I should get going. You probably don't want to be around me right now, and I feel like I'm just in the way," I say hesitantly. I know I have ended things very abruptly and unexpectedly for him, but the weight of my concerns about our growing relationship is just overwhelming.

"Well, whatever you want to do," Luke responds listlessly. I can tell he's angry with me, but he's not verbalizing it. Instead, he's continuing to clean, almost like I'm not here.

I pack up my bags from my second and final weekend at Luke's apartment. I don't want to go, but I also don't want the feelings we have for each other to override the decision we just made.  We leave his apartment, we get in his truck for him to drive me to my car, and I just feel a sudden sense of loneliness. I guess this is going to be harder than I thought. "Luke, I know I'm all over the place right now, but I do really enjoy your company.

my crazy #6

I can stay over – as long as you can agree that since we're just friends, nothing will happen between us," I propose.

"Yes, that's fine. I'd like you to stay and hang out as well," he says. I'm relieved, as I don't want to lose him as a friend.

He turns the car around, and we return to his apartment. Thankfully, we have a totally platonic night together, watching tennis and eating Chinese. It's amazing how we're able to go from intimacy to dormancy in a matter of hours. I suppose it's because, subconsciously, we had already started to drift apart. Plus, though our connection was very strong, in reality, it was only five weeks long. It should be relatively easy to sever ties after such a short affair. I even talk about maybe setting Luke up with a friend of mine, and he says he has someone else he is going to pursue since things with me have ended. Him pursuing someone else is a little hard to hear, but at the same time, I'm glad he has someone because he definitely seems to want to be in a relationship. He shares that the new girl is a tennis magazine model – how could I compete with that? He even shows me her photos, telling me she had been interested in him for some time, and he thinks now he'll give her a chance. Luke is a perfect gentleman the rest of the night, and as crazy as it sounds, we sleep together in bed as friends – with no benefits.

The next day, I have to update my girls. Especially Nadi, who loved him.

> **Me:** So.... hate to break hearts (since you gals love, love) but Luke and I decided to be friends yesterday. When he told me a couple wks ago that it bothered him that his wife wouldn't go to church with him and their daughter, I told him then we would be better off as friends bc I would not be different from his wife in that respect.... but he insisted we give it a try. And we did give it a try – we've definitely had fun spending the last 2 wknds together but yesterday he said it was strange for him leaving me in bed while he went to church... It was definitely new to me as well. I told him it won't get any better and while I think I could live with it bc I respect why he needs the structure of organized religion, I know how nice it is to share that experience with someone... and I'm not that person. He said maybe I could benefit from a trip to Isreal like the one he took to "answer some of my questions".... As you can see this would be a never-ending battle... even though our conversations were always light-hearted and respectful. I see us having a relationship like I do with "New Year's Mason," a great guy who I get along with and I love spending time with, but there's a fundamental issue that keeps us as just friends. ...So much for that Aruba wedding! ☺

Nadi: Mimi... I just knew he was the one for you. Are you sure you can't work thru the differences?? That sounds like the 20% that's workable.

Me: He and I are 90% right I'd say. But it would be quite a challenge for me to be with someone who is on the path to being somewhat fanatical about his faith.... even though I can relate bc I was once just like him. The harder part is knowing he'd be much better off with someone who isn't just supportive of his journey but on the road next to him. I know he wants someone by his side at church. It's really important to him and I know that's not me (anymore). When I was where he is, I totally wanted a guy like him who would read the bible and go to church with me, so I want that for him. Luke's a very passionate and committed person. He takes everything to the limit. So whether it's his fraternity where he's a former president, or fitness, where he's on a mission to lose more weight or even his beloved sport of tennis where he flies to the US Open almost every year.... he goes really hard in everything, and religion is no different. If I thought it was something we could work thru, I'd try, but seeing him on Sunday, after he came back from church, I knew being friends is the only answer... So, yes, it's unfortunate but that's life... Takes so much to make a successful relationship work, but I'm happy we can be friends.

After updating the girls, I text Luke.

Me: So, I was telling the girls we decided to be friends. I think they're sadder than we are lol. Gisela said we should just be "bed buddies" but as a good Christian man, that would not be moral ;-)

Luke: Wish I would've met you before Satan got a hold of you LOL.

Me: Haaaaaaaaa!! Yes agreed, I would've totally loved you 20 years ago lol. I was hesitant from the start bc of our religious differences, but I thought maybe….

Luke: Well back to the drawing board. Gonna do a google search to find Orlando speed dating locations now.

Me: I really wish it could've worked, so much good… If Jesus would just come down, He'd solve all our problems 😊

Luke: Jesus is already here. He's inside of you. Just talk to him and he will answer. I promise. No matter what people think, I will forever love the Lord. I will find the truth when I make the transition. If I do end up in heaven I'm going to ask the Angels in heaven to forgive you and to allow you entry because your heart is pure, genuine and filled with love.

Me: Awww thanks luv!! *kisses*

Luke: You're a good girl no doubt. Very high quality.

Me: Aww thanks babe, glad you feel that way about me. And the feeling is mutual, luv your heart and soul… oh and happy 1-month anniversary lol.

Luke: Now you're the green-eyed stalker's bae.

Me: Ha!

I tell Luke that I've been hearing from Leech again, and Luke tells me he is pursuing things with "tennis girl." We're officially moving on.

my crazy #7

One afternoon, while feeling a little nostalgic about our now-defunct relationship, I decide to take a look at Luke's Facebook page. Somehow, it hadn't dawned on me while we were dating to look at his page – perhaps, because we had friends in common, I didn't feel the need to do any "research" upon meeting him. What I find on his page in a matter of minutes tells me what it took me five weeks to find out. Luke is the type of person who posts multiple times a day, and it is usually about himself – every single distance run, church visit, tennis match, colonoscopy results, and – wait for it – every cemetery check-in is posted, religiously – no pun intended. Seeing tombstones and coffins with soldiers in them on his page makes me cringe. I can see that he is completely numb to his morbid side-job, though I suppose you would have to be to take on a job like that. Still, I feel that Luke's social media presence confirms that he is not the right guy for me. I conclude that Luke is a little OCD – when he loves something, he loves it hard, whether it's "the blood of Christ" he posts about, or his job, or fitness, or tennis, he does it at full speed, and you're going to know about it.

Nevertheless, I still feel Luke and I can remain friends. So, when he texts me a couple of Sundays later, I'm not surprised to hear from him, but I am surprised by what he says.

Luke: I just got home from a long weekend at my company's national conference. I won the President's Club Award. I so want to ask you to come over, but I know what it will lead to and I am very vulnerable right now. I mean bad. Was just thinking about intimate moments.

Me: Omg. I was so not expecting that message! Lol. Where is tennis girl? I was just about to get a mani/pedi and then I have a meeting with my mentee, but I can come over after to catch up… I'd keep us honest! Bc I still luv spending time with you.

Luke: Lol Sorry was just being honest. Maybe I shouldn't be so open with my thoughts. You're welcome to come by when you're done. Just know that it's ready. ☺

Me: Lol that's what's so great about you, you're open and honest. K, I'll plan to come by after… finals game is on tonight, too.

Back at Luke's apartment, I get comfortable on his couch and turn on the NBA finals game. "So, I've just got some work to catch up on, and I'll join you for the game in a little bit," Luke says.

"Oh, sure, no problem at all. You know I don't need to be entertained. I'm just going to relax," I say, remembering how much I like being at Luke's place. Making small talk while Luke sets up his computer, I ask, "So tell me about the conference... Where is your award?"

"Oh, it's here," he says, proudly lifting it off his desk for me to see.

"Wow, that's awesome," I say.

"Yeah, my boss was really proud. He drove me crazy all weekend, but it was a good conference. I learned a lot," he says. "How was your day?"

"It was nice. We had our graduation ceremony for our high-school mentees today. With the money we contributed, each graduate gets a laptop, so they were really happy." Luke had never expressed interest in getting involved with my charitable efforts, which was another reason he wasn't quite the right fit for me, but none of that matters now.

Luke proceeds to focus on completing his business expense reports while I watch the first quarter of the game on the other end of the couch, trying to be quiet so he can concentrate. He had picked up Chinese since he knew I was coming by, so we graze a little, but overall, it's just a relaxing afternoon watching basketball.

Luke finishes his work and closes his laptop. He puts away the dinner tray he had used and places the dishes in the sink. He walks across the room to turn off the lights, which feels a little odd since we aren't watching a movie, but it's okay.

Luke walks back over toward the couch, and within seconds, he's standing directly in front of me, while I'm still seated, and pulls down his pants. He is fully exposed as he grabs the back of my head. I immediately use my hand to stop him. "What are you doing, Luke? I told you that we're not going there," I say, feeling like I'm suddenly in a bad dream. Seeing that I'm not responding as he wants me to, he plunges his hand down the front of my dress, I suppose in an attempt to turn me on. "Luke, stop!" I scream, angrily pulling up my dress.

"You're right, you're right. I'm sorry," he says, almost like he had been snapped out of a trance. Deflated, he sits down next to me on the couch. His pants are still around his ankles.

"I thought we were just going to watch the game, and now you're turning off the lights, trying to be bad. You know we can't go there," I say, somewhat lightly because I'm hoping things don't escalate. I turn my attention back to the game, and all of a sudden, Luke puts his hand on the back of my neck and forces my face down toward his pelvis. "Luke!" I yell. "What are you doing? What's wrong with you?" I ask as I look him in the eye, still feeling the force of his hand on my neck though it is no longer there.

He doesn't respond. He is staring straight ahead, and in that instance, I get scared. It's the lifeless eyes I saw when we were on the trip and he walked passed me. The time I felt like he saw me, but at the same time, he didn't see me – like he was looking through me. This is the same empty look, but much worse. There's a darkness to his eyes, and I'm afraid that I might not get out of his apartment safely. For the first time in my life, I feel like I've put myself in harm's way – if he wants to over-power me and have his way with me, he certainly can. But then I start to think of all the friends we have in common, and how there's no way he would risk doing anything to me knowing that I would destroy his seemingly pristine reputation. I also think of how his Jesus statue is practically right above our heads. How could someone be such a believer and harm me? I just can't imagine he is capable of doing anything worse to me than what he's already done. "Luke, you're really scaring me. I think I need to go," I say as I go to get up from the couch.

"Wait, Mimi, don't leave. I'm going to stop, I promise," he responds.

The last time we were together, he was the perfect gentleman. And even when we were intimate, it was always respectful. I'm shocked that he's gotten aggressive with me out of the blue. While I could understand him having lustful feelings, I never thought he would forcefully try and have his way with me. I want to believe his son's mom made up the rape allegations, but after what I've experienced, I wonder if he has dark moments where he loses control and acts out. Perhaps that's why he clings to religion to keep him from slipping into that negative place – I'll never truly know. I should leave, but I decide to stay. Fortunately, Luke behaves the rest of the night, but he never owns his actions or apologizes. I feel like the Luke I met was his representative, and now I've seen his other side.

my crazy #8

A couple weeks go by, and we barely talk. I text Luke because I had left my favorite umbrella at his place and I was nearby. I ask him to bring it out to my car if I stop by his apartment and he obliges. "Hey, Mimi, how have you been?" he asks as he sets my umbrella in my passenger seat through the open window.

"I'm fine, but I have to tell you, I was really uncomfortable the last time I was here," I say, hoping it will trigger an apology from him. Instead, I get a blank stare. I continue. "You don't feel like what you did to me was inappropriate?"

"You're right, I'm sorry," he responds. But there is no emotion to his words, nor is any rationale provided. I don't feel his words are sincere at all but are just a way to satiate me. I stay silent, waiting for more of an explanation. "So, you know my dad and my brothers are coming in this weekend," he says, totally changing the subject.

I know any chance to salvage a piece of our short-lived friendship is really over now. I decide to just respond generically and go on my way. "Yes, I do remember your family coming in. I hope you all have a good weekend. I'm heading to Miami with the girls. I'll talk to you later," I say before driving off. I know there is no way I can be around Luke again.

Leech had squirmed his way back into my life over the last couple weeks, and when I tell him I'm heading to Miami for a film festival, he makes plans to attend as well. He seems happy to meet up with me, we have one great make-out session in my room (with our clothes on), and I never hear from him again after he leaves. I guess he wanted more – oh, well. It was doomed to fail eventually anyway. His voice alone was enough to put me to sleep.

Six months pass, and I do not see or talk to Luke until he reaches out via text to wish me a happy birthday and to invite me to dinner. I'm hesitant about going but decide to definitely not meet him after he texts me one night: 'go to my place – the door is open. LOL' It just reminds me that he can never take seriously the last night we were together, and I can't get past it without a true apology.

A month later, Luke sees via Facebook that we are at the same football game.

Luke: You're nowhere near me in the stadium, right?

Me: Not unless you're going to run across the field lol.

Luke: For a hug and kiss? Ummm…

Me: You're still on punishment…

Luke: Apparently. And I did nothing wrong.

Me: Wow.

Luke: ☺☺☺ I miss you.

Me: Whatever. You've had some libations apparently.

Luke: No. I do miss you. I enjoyed your company and conversation. I remember the fun times. You're focused on the drama. ☺ ☺ ☺

Me: I'm focused on you being aggressive with me the last time we were together.

Luke: I don't remember. Seriously.

Me: Interesting

Luke: I'm sorry.

Me: Thank you.

His text apology is really lost on me. I don't feel it is genuine whatsoever.

A month later, Luke reaches out to invite me to come to his new house.

Luke: When are you coming to visit me? Never?

Me: I really wanted us to be friends, but I don't feel you can see me that way. I'm honestly scared to be alone with you. That is why I pulled away.

Luke: Oh my. You scared of me huh? ☺ I don't bite.

The back-and-forth is pointless. I don't respond. A few months later, Luke sends me a Facebook invite to a birthday party he's hosting at his house for a friend. When I decline the invite, he immediately texts me asking why I can't come. I tell Luke it's because I'm not comfortable and because I feel we don't have a rapport. His response? He immediately blocks me on Facebook and deletes my number. Just in case I needed evidence of his abrupt and rash reactions, here it is. It seems he may be an officer, but he's certainly not a gentleman. It's time to end this trip to nowhere.

Take a Page from My Book

All that glitters is not gold. Just because someone "looks nice," and because so many people you trust tell you he is a good person, doesn't mean it's true. I have put myself in harm's way more times than I care to admit, and while I never would've thought Luke would get aggressive with me, I Should've Left as soon as I felt there was a risk that something bad would happen in his apartment that night. And there is definitely a case to be made for ending things with him when my intuition alarms noticed his emotional instability soon after we met. I always worry about hurting other people's feelings, and I have a strong curiosity to see relationships through, sometimes to my own detriment. Put yourself first, and don't put up with BS from anyone. Pay attention to the signs. Someone who is somewhat emotionally unstable is a ticking time bomb – it's only a matter of time before they explode.

Had to look beyond the picture-perfect times with "Paisley" and move on...

I Should've Left When...

Book of Flight

♡

Flight

TRAVEL BACK IN TIME TO 2009

"Mimi, let me introduce you to Torrance. You're both from Philly, so, I think you two should meet," says Annette. Annette is an older, well-respected woman in the Orlando community who I've known for years. I imagine that Torrance must be a decent single catch if Annette wants to introduce me to him. Torrance certainly looks like my type: tall, nice suit, attractive. Not that men with my physical preference have worked for me in the past .

"Torrance has been helping our company with a financial deal, so he's in town for the week from Philly," says Annette, completing her introduction. *Ooh, he sounds smart and successful. Double high-five Annette!*

"Hello, Mimi. It's nice to meet you," Torrance says, extending his hand. We're mingling at a private social club's holiday party in downtown Orlando. It's nice to have a fresh, out-of-town face here, especially one from my hometown.

Everyone is dressed for the holiday season, and the social club crowd is lively and sophisticated. However, with Torrance being about 6'4" (plus the loud music and dancing), it's tough to carry on a conversation. We manage to get in one of the quintessential questions one asks when meeting someone from their hometown. "So, where did you go to high school?" he asks.

"Oh, I went to Central," I respond.

"No way," says Torrance. "So did I. What class number?" he asks.

"I was 254." We realize he is about 10 years older, but it's still a pretty cool commonality given that we're meeting over 1,000 miles away from our alma mater.

After another minute or so of small talk, we exchange business cards and part ways, but we agree to keep in touch. As the night ends, I feel like I've met a decent new dating prospect, albeit a long-distance one. But for some reason, I don't have excitement or butterflies. There's just something about Torrance that doesn't do it for me – however, I can't call it yet.

LAYOVER UNTIL 2016

My lack of excitement about Torrance, plus the lack of social media's broad usage back in 2009 when we met, caused a seven-year time lapse before I reconnected with him. Yes, seven whole years.

Scrolling through Facebook randomly one Saturday afternoon, I see Torrance's profile photo as a "person you may know." I can't remember much about Torrance except the night we met through Annette at the holiday party, and maybe one date soon after, at a hibachi restaurant by my house. I know seven years can erase a lot of memory, but I faintly remember him being in my bedroom that night. Maybe something went down that was very lackluster  (and clearly forgettable). I feel like I remember him having a small package and an inability to deliver, but I really can't say for sure. My curiosity compels me to send Torrance the suggested Facebook friend request and see what happens.

my crazy #8

It's July 4th weekend 2016, and after two defunct near-relationships this year with Vegas and Aruba Luke, I decide to visit my safe place with Mason. I head back to the beach with him for the patriotic holiday. The last time we were together was for New Year's – pre-Vegas and pre-Luke.

"What so funny?" asks Mason, who is relaxing in his arm-chair in his South Florida apartment.

I'm across from him lounging on the sofa. "Uh, well..." I struggle with deciding whether to explain my sudden laughter to Mason. Torrance has just accepted my Facebook friend request, causing me to laugh out loud.

Mason and I have an interesting relationship. On the positive side, we share a lot in common:

✓ We met on a mutual friend's Facebook post a couple years ago (ironically, another Facebook connection like Torrance). Mason and I shared similar views about moving south to Florida for the love of warmer weather and doing so rather quickly.

✓ Neither of us has nor wants children.

✓ We share a few mutual friends.

Given our commonalities, we decide to get to know each other better.

Mason requests our first date, then cancels when he's unexpectedly hospitalized with high-blood-pressure (he even sends me his date-stamped hospital bracelet to prove he wasn't trying to ditch me). A few weeks later, he makes it up to me with a sexy date at his condo's pool. He packs an awesome cooler of treats and drinks for our pool date, which inevitably leads to his bedroom for a hot makeout session, but nothing more. I conclude after our first date that I like Mason. However, he doesn't initiate date number two, so I take the reins.

One Friday night, not long after we met, I invite Mason out to an after-work dance party at an intimate lounge. I know he loves music, and I thought it'd be a fun night out together. However, Mason abruptly leaves at 8:00, telling me that while he loves the music, he doesn't like crowds or dancing. I realize then that Mason isn't the right guy for me long-term because he gets easily exhausted in social settings. But I feel we can be friends.

Not long after our botched dance night, Mason moves three hours away to Boca Raton for work. We don't see each other for over a year, but we stay loosely connected through good ol' Facebook. Mason, who is a pure introvert and rarely picks up the phone, actually calls to wish me happy birthday in December, and about a week later, as New Year's is approaching and I have nothing exciting to do, I decide to spend it with Mason. I know I'll enjoy spending time with him because he does have a fun personality, and I also trust him.

I'm attracted to Mason physically, though he has a smaller frame than I prefer. But we always have good conversations, and we get along great. We have a fun New Year's Eve on the beach with his friend and his friend's wife, listening to old music, sipping tequila, and sharing great food that his friend grills fresh on the beach. On New Year's Eve night, after one too many tequilas, Mason and I have a wild night together in bed. He has a lot of energy and is very catering, but it is our first and only time closing the deal. While it was quite fun, I make it clear to Mason that another night rolling around in his bed is not in the cards. He is entirely too introverted for my crazy life, I try not to have physical relationships with guys with whom I know I have no future. I know how easily I can get caught up. Plus, visualizing regularly spending my nights on the couch with Mason, eating Oreo Thins, drinking almond milk, and watching Netflix just won't do it for me. Although I do enjoy Mason's kitchen skills, and there are women who would kill for a man who likes to stay home and cook, I know it's not ideal for me.

Now, seven months after our New Year's rendezvous, it's a July 4th weekend, with no "fireworks." Mason and I are just friends, with a little flirtation thrown in.

I finally explain my sudden outburst to Mason while I'm sitting on his couch, knowing he likely doesn't want to hear about me and another guy – but also, if we are truly just friends, he should be able to take it. "So, Facebook suggested this guy to me as a friend a couple weeks ago. I haven't seen him in seven years. Heck, I don't even remember what happened with him," I say to Mason. Thankfully, Mason is unmoved and continues to watch the OJ Simpson 30 for 30 documentary that we're addicted to. I proceed to message Torrance back from Mason's couch.

Torrance: Hi MiMi

Me: Hey, how are you?

Torrance: Are you MiMi Mansfield from Philly?

Me: [*Ah, he remembers me – or did he just see that on my FB?*] Lol yes, it's on my fb.

Torrance: I'm not on FB... this is some message app. I'm not too FB savvy. Is this MiMi from Johnny's dodge ball league?

Me: [*Wth?!* Clearly, he's not FB savvy and doesn't understand the connection to FB Messenger. *And dodge ball league? Never.*] Lol no you met me in Orlando

Torrance: Ahhh... now I remember... Central High grad, right?

Me: Lol yes

Torrance: Smile... lol. Any chance you're up in Philly for the 4th?

Me: Ha, I'm in Florida.

Torrance: Oh okay. I've actually started working on a couple of deals in FL and I'm looking at office space down there in Sarasota.

Me: Ooh I love it there. My favorite restaurant is Selva, been going there on vacation for the last 5 summers.

Torrance: I have seen that restaurant… I like the whole area. Holding a lot of meetings at the Ritz… but it's time to take it to another level now. I'm looking at renting… down to two apartments. I should probably get a woman's opinion b4 I make my final decision.

Me: Lol yes, that's a good idea

Torrance: Will you tell me when you're planning on being in Sarasota… I'd be happy to take you to Selva if your schedule permits.

Me: Wow, so kind of you. I'm pretty flexible. This month or next?

Torrance: Both! Lol

Me: Ha! Ok, you have your flights booked yet or no?

Torrance: Not yet… I'm flexible, 254.

Me: Ha, good memory, yes, Central High, 254th class.

Torrance: I have to be honest… I wrote it down in my contact for you.

Me: Haaaa! I was going to say. Considering you didn't recognize me from my FB messenger photo, I was surprised you remembered my graduating class number. You do recall coming to my house, right? [Although I wasn't sure he came to my house, I figured I should ask with confidence.]

Torrance: I did? Refresh my memory… did I pick you up for dinner or something?

Me: Ha. We went to dinner down the street from my house at a hibachi place. You may have picked me up.

Torrance: Nice. Well I feel we reconnected for a reason. Do you think Sarasota is a good area to buy in? I'm looking for a place with good restaurants… access to the water (boating and fishing more than just beach)…

an airport easy to get in and out of without a ton of kids around. An older crowd is okay... my Ybor City days are done... lol I would like a place that may grow some... vs just a retirement community. Will you show me around?

Me: I'm no expert but happy to show you what I know.

I feel like I should wrap up my conversation with Torrance since, after all, I am at Mason's apartment as his guest. I tell Torrance we can talk later, and I continue my friendly weekend with Mason of watching TV on the couch and then going to the beach for the 4th.

When I return home to Orlando, Mason and I retreat to our regular pattern of virtually no communication outside of the occasional Facebook comment, and things take off with Torrance.

BUCKLE-UP

Torrance telling me about his business meetings at the Ritz, offering me dinner at one of my favorite restaurants, and mentioning his love for boating definitely gives me the impression that his financial consulting business is a success. And looking at his Facebook photo, he still looks good after seven years. I admit I am intrigued to see where this goes.

I tell Torrance that I can't remember why we lost touch - heck, he seems like a great catch: early 50s, never married, and a son in college. I suggest he and I take our messenger conversation to the phone. Both of us still have each other's numbers stored from seven years ago - thank you, Samsung.

Torrance: I don't remember why we lost touch either! I don't recall anything negative... only good and positive vibes from U! I'm up for a phone convo whenever you are... I am flexible!

We decide to jump on the phone Sunday night. "Hello?" Torrance says as he answers my call.

"Hey there. It's Mimi. How are you?" I ask.

"I'm doing fine. You're getting ready for bed?" Torrance asks.

"I am," I respond, with some hesitation. The more Torrance speaks, the more I hear a somewhat effeminate voice. *This can't be real; maybe he just needs to clear his throat.*

"So, I was just on the phone with my good friend and client about coming down to Sarasota again. I'm planning on that first weekend of August; will you be around then?" Torrance asks. It's official. Torrance sounds like Michael Jackson circa 1975.

Why is his voice so soft?! Sheesh! Always something. But I try to look past traits that cannot be controlled, which is why I have dated the overweight, the short, and maybe now, the "soft-spoken" man. "Uh, yes, I'll be around that weekend," I respond. "I'm actually planning to visit friends in Naples that weekend, but perhaps I can swing by Sarasota on my way back home," I say. Reconnecting briefly with Torrance over dinner while passing through Sarasota would make sense. There'll be no reason for anything more than just dinner. We conclude our phone conversation, and though I can't understand why I don't recall this voice issue from before, I'm still somewhat interested in seeing where things go.

The next day, Torrance follows up with a nice message.

turn on #1

Torrance: My plan is to get to know you better. I would like to have some conversations every now and again. I enjoyed our chat last nite. You have a calming voice and a cute laugh.

Me: Awww thank you! [*Too bad I can't return the positive voice compliment.*] How was your day?

Torrance: I had a productive day. How was the meeting you mentioned?

Me: It was good... had a call for a summer camp my friends and I do here. It's a girl's summer camp that starts next week for 4 weeks

Torrance: Very cool! Do you plan the activities for the camp... or just help out there?

Me: Thanks! I help plan activities, get donations and volunteer.

Torrance: Impressive.... most impressive! Can you share more info about the camp? I have a STEM program that might be of interest to you.

Me: Oh ok! Sure, check out our site, Tgicamp.org.

Torrance: Looks like an amazing endeavor! I'd like to help...

Me: Gosh well aren't you the best! We are most in need of financial sponsors and drivers.

Torrance: Can I come down and offer my driver services for the young ladies in exchange for dinner with one of the women who run the camp?!? 😊

Me: Haaaaaaaa! We need a driver for 4 weeks

Torrance: Will work for food

Me: Lol! I'm sure you don't have that kind of flexibility. Plus, 4 weeks of driving teenage girls? You'd need me to take YOU to dinner lol

Torrance: I'm sure I do... I'm planning my move to Florida anyway remember?

Me: True. But you'd have to be here by Monday. (I'm testing Torrance as I'm sure he's just joking.)

Torrance: Well... I was hoping that U might slip a meal or two for me into the mix. Home-cooked preferably... 😊

Me: Lol well for 4 weeks of driving that would be the least we could do. But I know you're not serious.

Torrance: Do you have a couch I could crash on downstairs?

Me: Lol there's no way you're prepared to move in with a virtual stranger for 4 weeks. Not to mention, for the driver, since it is young girls, we'd need it to be someone we really know.

Torrance: Oh... so you're telling me after 7 years you don't know me well enough? Humph 😠

Me: Lmao. We haven't even spent 7 hours together lol

Torrance: Hmmm... well there was the party where we met... that was a couple of hours... then dinner... at least an hour... then our close encounter... at least 5 hours 😎... so we should be waaayy past 7!! Smile

Me: Haaaaaaaa!!!! That did make me laugh lol!

Torrance: Good! Want me to come down this weekend for an interview? U can do a background check on me... I had to get fingerprinted and everything to get my Florida insurance license.

Me: I'm still feeling like you're joking about coming... I'm not busy this wknd so totally your call.

Me: Assuming you'd get a hotel.

Torrance: I could get a hotel this weekend... but if I pass... would you make me get one for the entire 4 weeks?

Me: I can't imagine having someone stay with me even a few nights that I don't really know. Just not a wise move for a single woman, right?

Torrance: I agree! Let me think this thru...

Me: Ok [*There's no way he's serious, right?*]

intuition
alarm #9

Torrance: Maybe I could crash with my friend Russell or something... If you are in a pinch... I could drive next week.

Me: I'm surprised you're even able to uproot so quickly.

Torrance: I am single, and my son would luv to have the condo to himself!

Me: Ha, I bet!

Torrance: So... since you aren't offering room or board... are there any perks to this job at all?

Me: Haaaaaaaa! Lol the ideal volunteer will do this job out of the kindness of their hearts, not bc they want anything in return 😊

Torrance: Hmmm... I want to be ideal... but your face on my phone all the time is blurring my vision! 😵

Me: Awww! Guess my face didn't work 7 years ago but it's on fiyah now! Ha

Torrance: It did... clearly... you got me into your bedroom! Lol I'm just more focused now and this IM thang you have working has me en fuego! Hahaha

Me: Haaaaaaaa!!!

Torrance: Let's keep talking... whenever you want. Get to know each other better and hang out soon!!

We move on from the camp driver conversation, and Torrance and I continue communicating daily over the next couple weeks. He thinks he'll be able to make a quick weekend trip from Philly to Orlando to see me. "Between offering to help me with my charity, understanding and relating to my beliefs, and hearing how well-connected you are, you could be missing a limb and I'd still be intrigued," I tell Torrance. "Oh, and yeah, my other thing: someone who communicates well and doesn't disappear... You're checking all my boxes all of a sudden."

"Is that so?" Torrance responds.

"Yes," I say, laughing, before reminding him that we're just friends for now, but he should book his flight for this weekend. "Flight and hotel that is," I tell him, as a reminder that he can't stay in my house.

intuition alarm #10

The next morning, Torrance calls. "Hey, Mimi, I'm sorry. I can't get this financial analysis done in time to make it to Orlando this weekend, but we should go to Paris together at some point," he says. Well, I was looking forward to finding out sooner than later if there is something off with Torrance, but it'll have to wait for now. At least he's speaking my language talking about taking a trip. I live for adventure.

"I do need a Paris do-over," I tell Torrance, thinking to myself about my Parisian Valentine's trip years ago that went very south.

"I also probably shouldn't come down this weekend, so I can get my Paris pocket change correct! I've got to get more business going down there so I can afford all the hotel nights and taking you out!" he says. I'm sure Torrance is teasing about the money; it's nice that he's being humble. Given all the business deals he has told me about, it definitely seems he is doing well.

So, instead of visiting me in Orlando, Torrance stays in Philly and golfs with his business contacts. "Have a good game today," I tell Torrance.

"Well, if you want to impress a true golf player, like myself, in the future, you'll want to refer to it as a *round* of golf," he says.

"Oh, wow, well thank you. I love someone who can teach me things. I appreciate that," I say.

Over the next couple weeks, Torrance and I get to know each other better.

We realize we are aligned on budgeting.

Torrance: I hang with some ballers at times and they roll outside my means... especially with a son in college. My cash flow is inconsistent at times... so, I have to be disciplined and not do everything I want to do right now!! U included... but starting in September... things should be mo betta!!

Me: Well good, let's get it! But even when you have it, I'll encourage you to save it. I am really uncomfortable with overspending. I splurge every now and again, usually on clothes for trips, but I almost always buy on discount. I'm a big Ross shopper lol. Spending a lot on food and drink often would pain me. You can call me Frugal Francesca.

Torrance: I hear ya, Frugal Franny. Lol. But deal... I think we will be wonderful for one another.

We also share a love of foreign languages.

Torrance: De nada... Muchas gracias... Oui oui…

Me: Lol si

Torrance: I gave you Portuguese... Spanish then French... I'm trying to expand in all 3. Any French you can help me with would be much obliged...

Me: D'accord. Means okay. Thanks to my 13 years of French in the Philly public school system. Who says our tax dollars aren't working?

Torrance: Awesomeness! 😊 I'd much rather learn slowly... from U. Keep it coming... por favor...

We even love the same types of programs.

Me: How's your afternoon?

Torrance: I'm watching Made in America-OJ with my son

Me: Oh my goodness you don't know how addicted I am to that series. [Of course, I feel no need to mention that I watched it on Mason's couch a few weeks ago.]

And lastly, and super-important to me, we have a shared love of old-school music.

Me: I'm at Clearwater beach having lunch with my friend Sasha and her husband. I've got a glass of Pinot Noir and the live band is playing Private Eyes, I'm in heaven.

Torrance: Hall & Oates! Classic!!

Me: Yes! Very good. One of my favorite bands.

Torrance: Ditto. Plus, I also enjoy wine. I bet we can share some nice wine selections together. We have so much in common... and enuf things are different to keep it interesting!!

Me: Lol exactly. I like commonalities.

I call Torrance after we've been mostly texting for a month. I decide to see where he is with scheduling a trip to Florida. "You know, I've been wanting to get away soon since it is the heart of summer right now," I say. "Well... let me know when you figure it out... I want to see you."

"Whenever... wherever... whatever!" he says. Not exactly the answer I'm looking for since I want HIM to take the lead, but ok.

"Hey, it's up to you. I'm ready for you to come to Florida at least. You just have to book your flight," I tell Torrance.

"Just a flight?!?" he asks.

"Well, I mean at least a flight to lock down the date," I respond.

"Ok... whatever you say, boss. I will be a good boy."

"Nice. That means you'll book a trip soon?"

"I can crash on your couch?"

Sheesh, this guy is really trying to get in my house. "When do you want to come?" I ask, before realizing my Freudian slip. "Come to visit!" I add.

"Are you flirting with me, Ms. Mansfield?" he asks, with laughter.

"Ha, I'm just trying to keep the convo above board."

"Ok, good... because I'm going to be a good boy when I see you, so you know you can feel comfortable with me."

turn on #1

"I appreciate that." I don't know where this is going, but I do love when a guy is forward-looking and gives me some potential excitement for the future. I might just be able to get over his effeminate voice if we continue to get along this well.

Torrance doesn't call very often and usually doesn't answer when I call, but he agrees to a video call one Saturday night. I'm hoping we'll finally pin down a trip. "Evening, sunshine. You're looking quite beautiful," Torrance says as he answers my call. He pretty much looks like I remember from seven years ago, maybe just slightly grayer.

"Why, thank you. I'm cozy and ready for bed," I say before looking more closely at my image and realizing part of my areola is showing. My nighttime tank top had conveniently floated south. "Oh, my goodness. You weren't going to tell me, were you?" I say lightly, adjusting my top and pulling the sheet up on me.

"Well, I wasn't fully sure what I was seeing, but now I'm turned on," Torrance says.

"Ha, I can imagine, but we're not about to have that type of call, so let's change the subject... How was your day?" I ask, pivoting the conversation.

"You know me – I played 18 holes today with the guys, and we went out for lunch and drinks after," Torrance responds.

"Ah, of course, your favorite pastime," I say.

"So, listen, Mimi, I have business in Sarasota next weekend. Do you think you'll be able to make it down to see me?" he asks.

"Oh, cool. Yes, remember I'm heading a couple hours south of Sarasota to Naples. My friend Tindall and her husband are renting a catamaran Saturday. Maybe you can join us?" I ask.

"Hmm, I'm not sure I can swing Naples, but I most definitely want to see you on Sunday if you can make it to Sarasota. I'm going to be staying with a friend, but maybe we can go to your favorite restaurant in the area you mentioned."

"Ok, I should be able to make that happen."

"Hey, I'm really enjoying this video chat. I've never done this before. I'm very visual, and seeing you seems to tranquilize me. I'd love if you could send me a photo to keep me satiated," he says.

turn off #10

Oh, boy. In my head, I can hear my friends, like Giselle for example, who absolutely hate sending photos to guys. Giselle will cut a guy off just for asking lol. Luckily for Torrance, I don't mind it. He claims he never goes on Facebook, sooo text it is.

"Ok, I'll text you a couple photos when we get off the phone. Just let me know when you've booked your flight."

Me: [I text him a bikini shot and one in a gown from my friend Mara's wedding in Mexico.]

Torrance: I've never been to Mexico... perhaps I can accompany you for your next wedding there...

turn off #10

Torrance: Now can you send me a backshot? 👍

Me: No backshot! Smh. Come and see it for yourself... can't beat the real thing...

And this is why my friend Giselle doesn't send photos to guys. They get carried away. But I'm going to let it slide.

Torrance: I just went direct to Frontier Air's website, instead of CheapOair, but both sites keep freezing. Quite frustrating... I will try to book one more time in the morning and then I will just call them.

Torrance's technology challenges are starting to remind me of Leech in Aruba. 😒 I'll blame his "maturity." At this point, I'm just going to hope he's not pseudo-catfishing me, because I've never seen someone take so long to book a flight (I say "pseudo" since we have met before and video chatted).

Me: Well just keep in mind Frontier costs extra for baggage, that's why I ♥ Southwest.

Torrance: U have heavy baggage fees too... but I'm trying to deal with it.

Me: Lol, good one. Well, I'm trying to unpack my baggage. As long as you treat me well, I won't accumulate any more.

Torrance: Lol I will try... I think you have more baggage than shoes tho!! Lmao

Me: Ha! Yes, but I acknowledge my baggage and you'd be pressed to find a grown woman who has been dating men who doesn't have baggage of some kind. And yes, you're supposed to be good bc we're supposed to be friends!

Torrance: Just bring your sweet self to Sarasota asap... Can you come Saturday night instead of just Sunday?

Me: If you book a hotel ahead of time and it's somewhere I'm comfortable staying then ok. I'm 4 stars and over only – sorry, yes, I'm picky. And I need my own room – I can pay for mine if you reserve.

Torrance: Ok... snooty booty. Lol 😎

Me: You're the one who told me you stayed at the Ritz during one of our first conversations.

Torrance: I've also stayed at a Hampton and Holiday Inn... but that's just me. It's all good...

Me: If you're asking me to change my plans and spend the night with you Saturday (in separate beds), clearly you have a plan and it's not for me to drive up 2 hours from Naples to Sarasota and hope to find a place to stay last min.

Me: I stayed at a Hampton Inn in Tally last week for our summer camp. It was fine, but they can be hit-or-miss, and I don't like rolling dice. I also would never stay at a Hampton on vacation...

Torrance: Okay Mimi... gotcha. I don't have a plan yet... It was just an idea so far... I've got to develop a plan.

READY FOR TAKEOFF

The next morning, Torrance texts me.

Torrance: Guess what?

Me: Lol what?

Torrance: I just booked my flight! 🌐

Me: Lmao! Great! Glad you're finally legit. And a friendly reminder, no promises of close encounters next weekend. In fact, my goal is to wait a year before having any.

Torrance: Okay... no problemo... no pressure! Wait, you're waiting a year... from when... one of your ex's?!?

Me: Lmao I haven't decided but know I want to wait a while...

Torrance: Okay.

During the week after Torrance books his flight, he doesn't provide any details on his schedule or where he's staying, so I go with the flow, though the lack of details is driving me a tad crazy.

On Friday, he texts me again.

Torrance: Just landed in Sarasota... Yay!!

Me: Sweet. Ok, so when did you want to see me?

Torrance: Tonight... lol. Look at where I'm staying... This is the place I'm renting on the golf course for $200/night!!!... by myself. We could have a house like this one day!! ☺

Torrance: Can you come hang out with me here?

Me: That's crazy, how did you get that? My friends are wanting me to stay and party with them in Naples Sat nte but that house sure looks nice.

Torrance: If you want to hang out with your friends... I completely understand. We can connect on Sunday if you want.

Me: If we can play it by ear, that'd be ideal. My only reservation about coming there is that you could be an axe murderer and I don't know it.

Torrance: Really?!?

Me: Lol. I mean, I don't REALLY know you. And you appear in town and suddenly send me a photo of a house. I haven't talked to you... I just feel disconnected.

Torrance: I understand... Perhaps you should stay with your friends. No worries...

Me: You didn't tell me how you got the house. You have to understand that it's different than mtg you at a hotel.

Torrance: U didn't ask me...

Me: I did ask above, "how did you get that?" And I called you twice yesterday to catch up, but you didn't answer.

turn off #11

Torrance: I thought it might make you more comfortable... not less. Do you think it's easier to get away with a murder at a hotel... or a place like this?!? Duh...

Me: Hotels have cameras and security. You have to understand this from my perspective. Last we left off, you told me you were staying with your friend and then asked me to book something. Then you send me photos of a house that you're staying in alone. I just needed the pieces of the puzzle to fit.

Torrance: I understand now... Things changed because my friend I was staying with told me I could get the whole place for $200 a night but had to get it for the weekend, so I just went for it. I figured we could have separate showers/rooms that you could lock, and we could really chillax in a stress-free environment. This is from upstairs. I wanted to impress you... Sorry I scared you away...

turn on #5

Me: Looks awesome. I'm quite impressed. Ritz what? Ritz who? Lol

Torrance: Nope... U hurt my feelings... Go hang out with your friends... humph

Me: Haaaaaaaa! I'm sorry. I really was like, is he trying to lure me into some set-up?

Me: Like, come to this address and I'll be waiting for you.

Torrance: Set-up for what?

Me: Hopefully you can understand that I just needed the gaps filled in.

Me: And I know I was hurting your feelings and I'm sorry. I just needed to understand. Listen, we single girls have to be careful. Could've been any kind of set-up... sexual, financial, etc.

Me: I know, I know, me and my baggage. Mind is always racing. Doesn't help that I work in fraud so always thinking of the worst-case scenario.

Torrance: U sought ME out... How do I know U aren't cray cray?!? Lol

Me: Right, all this time I was catfishing you and I'm really Mimi from Johnny's dodge ball league in Philly, lol. Jk. Too funny.

Torrance: Well, I still want to hang out with you... It's just that nothing is going down in the DM... So we can just enjoy each other's company.

Me: Lmao right.

Torrance: I'm down to compromise... You are the one with all the rules and regulations

Me: Lol I'll be good, promise.

Torrance: Hmmm we shall see. Well just let me know if you change your mind and decide not to come tomorrow night.

Me: I'll plan to come visit you in Sarasota Saturday evening now instead of just Sunday.

I wake up early Saturday morning to make the three-hour drive down to Tindall's house for the noon catamaran ride. However, we get to the boat slip, and there is a mechanical failure, so the ride is canceled – buzz kill. I text Torrance.

Me: You must've jinxed our boat ride so I'd come see you sooner.

Torrance: Awww... Sorry to hear that... but U know you want to come see me asap... So stop frontin'! Lol

I can't deny that I'm actually looking forward to finally hanging out with Torrance again after seven years. We've had a few disagreements, but I feel it's in part due to most of our conversation being over text. I hope he's really a good guy. And knowing that he went out of his way to book the house for me, I decide to head his way sooner than initially planned. After lunch in Naples with Tindall and her husband, I hug them goodbye, and make the two-hour drive back to Sarasota – at least it's on my way home.

I pull into the Sarasota golf community and, wow, it is stunning. While I'm used to golf communities (Orlando is filled with them), this one in Sarasota is especially gorgeous. Behind the gates, I find a very natural environment, sprawling with 100-year-old pine and oak trees. The community is also peppered with million-dollar homes.

I call Torrance. "Hey there, I just got through the guard gate. This place is beautiful – thank you for inviting me!" I say.

"And, see? You thought I was sending you to a trap house," he laughs. Torrance guides me through the winding roads to meet him at his rented eight-bedroom home.

Pulling up to the home, Torrance doesn't look quite as good as I remember, nor does he look as good as in the photos he sent recently, but it's probably just because his hairline has receded and the additional gray is more prominent. Luckily for him, I can look past physical flaws – heck, anything is better than Vegas.

"I made it!" I say as I get out the car.

"You did, Mimi. It's good to see you," he says, giving me a hug. His voice is still soft in person, but I feel I can manage.

I go to grab my overnight bag out of the backseat. Out of the corner of my eye, I catch Torrance sneaking a picture of me from behind. He's not the quickest with the phone, I see. I decide not to call him out. Figure it's best not to rock the boat before we even begin our time together. Plus, a small part of me is flattered he's snapping photos of me.

We walk into the house, and it looks like it did in the photos: high-end, country-club inspired décor, with rich, dark wood furniture. He takes me on a full tour, six bedrooms upstairs, and he shows me around the first floor. "Let me show you one of the other bedrooms where you can stay. I'm in the room down to the left, and you can stay over here to the right," Torrance says as we walk around the first floor. He escorts me into a large master bedroom, decorated Tommy Bahama style, with a dark wood headboard and clean white linens.

"This looks great, Torrance. Thanks," I say.

"I'm glad you're pleased."

It's 4:00 in the afternoon, so a little early for dinner. I'm exhausted from driving most of the day away, so I ask Torrance, "Do you mind if I take a power nap?"

turn on #5

"Not at all. Why don't you take a nap, and when you wake up, there's a sushi restaurant at a really nice plaza nearby. I remember you like sushi. We're a little too far from your favorite restaurant."

"Sushi nearby sounds awesome."

The long day of driving, coupled with my fatigue from Mother Nature's monthly gift, knocks me out for much longer than I plan. I don't wake up until after 8:00. I was really looking forward to exploring this part of Sarasota in the daylight, but so much for that. I walk down to Torrance's room to see why he didn't wake me up. I find that he, too, is asleep, so I nudge him. "Now I see why you didn't wake me up," I say, laughing.

"Oh, wow, what time is it?" he asks, rubbing his eyes.

"It's after 8:00; it's almost dark," I say, sitting down on the foot of his bed.

"I'm sorry, Mimi. I didn't mean to fall asleep. Are you hungry? What would you like to do?" he asks.

"Well, I had a good lunch in Naples before I left, so actually, I'm not too hungry," I say.

"I have some light snacks in the fridge, and I have some adult beverages here for you if you'd like to partake," Torrance offers.

"Hmm, well, as long as you don't Bill Cosby me, I guess I can have a drink," I say teasingly.

"Bill Cosby's legacy is ruined," Torrance says.

"Yes, and rightfully so," I respond.

"Fair enough. Let's head into the kitchen," Torrance says.

I pull up a bar stool while Torrance rummages through the full-sized Sub-Zero refrigerator. He places his small collection of cheeses, meats, and crackers on the counter for me, and pulls out glasses for me to make a drink with Patron. *Definitely stronger than I would prefer, but I'll pour lightly.* I pour drinks for both of us: Patron with a fruit punch he bought – yes, we are from Philly.

Torrance asks, "So, what do I have to do to keep you being fantastique with me?"

"Well, honesty, communication, and intelligence, I would say are my top three," I tell Torrance while taking a sip of the cocktail concoction.

"I can handle those," Torrance says, flipping through the channels and finding the Queens of Comedy. Great choice for what has turned into a low-key evening in.

"How about you? What are some of your favorite things?" I ask him as I get comfortable in the leather tufted barstool.

"I would say 'close encounters' [air quotes], food, music, and sports."

"Ah, yes. Go Eagles!" I respond, giving him a high five.

"How about pet peeves?" Torrance asks as we continue to get reacquainted.

"Hmmm, the one that comes to mind after spending five hours on the road today is bad drivers! I can't stand people who stay in the fast lane. Just pass cars, then move right! And use a turn signal!" I say, laughing.

"Oh, well mine is people who talk with their mouth full!" Torrance says as our drinks are settling in and we're getting a little more relaxed.

"Ugh, that is the worst. That or the lip-smacker," I say, and we laugh in unison.

I'm about to chime in with another getting-to-know-you question when a huge flying roach dives right over the bar and onto the white wall in front of us. "Oh my gosh!" I yell, jumping up from the stool. Yes, I'm from Philly, and I live in Florida, but I absolutely abhor roaches. And while they can definitely come out anywhere, even an eight-bedroom house nestled in a ritzy golf community, I have to admit it was the furthest thing from my mind.

"Oh, Mimi, you're scared of these things? This is nothing. I've got it," Torrance says. He takes a swing at the roach, but the roach wins, practically teleporting to the foyer within seconds. Torrance goes after it again and thankfully wins the second battle by using his shoe.

"Oh, my goodness. I'm so glad you caught that thing, but now I'm afraid to sleep. What if there are more?" I say, realizing how crazy this sounds. But what can I say? I'm really a bit uncomfortable now.

"Well, Mimi, why don't you come to my room? I've been in there all day, and I know there's nothing in there," Torrance suggests.

Well, this is convenient for him. So much for avoiding the "close encounter." But I genuinely don't feel like I'll be able to sleep alone in this big ol' house.

We finish our evening snacks and drinks and head into Torrance's bedroom. I turn to place my phone on the nightstand. As I look down, I see another roach! Thankfully, this time, it's a dead one. "Oh, my goodness, Torrance. It's another bug on the floor," I say.

He goes over to pick it up. "Ok, would you rather go to your room?" he asks.

my crazy #5

"Yeah, maybe," I say, though at this point, you can call me Goldilocks because I don't feel comfortable anywhere. We climb in my bed, and the good ol' Patron starts to kick in. I'm feeling a little frisky all of a sudden and am thankful for Mother Nature's lovely gift, which will undoubtedly keep me safe in this precarious situation.

"I haven't gotten a chance to tell you, but I do really appreciate you securing this house for the weekend," I say, reaching over across the huge king-size bed to give Torrance our first intimate hug. I feel like he has earned a kiss, and his full-sized lips, though they could be moister for my taste, are pulling me in. I kiss Torrance, and it really is like the first time. If something happened in bed seven years ago, I have no recollection of it. And this time doesn't feel much different – I doubt it will be memorable. There are no sparks, but my inner bad girl lures me into climbing on top of Torrance, trying to spark something, though we are still fully clothed. Still, something about our encounter just doesn't feel exciting or natural – it's just off. Maybe it's roach-gate, or maybe I still sense that he isn't masculine enough for me, but I'm not feeling the heat. And Torrance, staying true to his promise to be good, doesn't initiate a thing, so I roll onto my back and we agree to watch a movie, which he falls asleep on after about 20 minutes.

I wake up the next morning and realize that at some point, Torrance went back to his bedroom. I must've scared him straight because he couldn't have been more of a gentleman. Almost reminds me of Vegas, who was not forward at all. Or another guy I dated long ago – I call him Tampa – who slept in bed with me like I was his sister. On one hand, I appreciate a man being a gentleman, especially on the heels of Aruba Luke, but a lack of assertiveness can make you question if a man is straight or if he's just not that into you. Can't really call it.

I text Torrance that I'm heading for a morning shower and will come see him shortly. I'm pretty anxious to get out of this place and back home. I spread my toiletries out on the large counter and get into the shower. The shower has nice natural light from a high window, and I'm getting into a Zen mode from the spa-like faucet. I close my eyes for a moment, letting the warm water run over me. I take a deep breath, feeling thankful that everything with Torrance has gone alright. As I open my eyes, I see another flying roach on the handicap chair by my leg. I scream as I jump out of the shower and grab a towel. I am so over this place! I gather my toiletries, hoping nothing has crawled inside them, and head over to Torrance's shower. "Torrance, I need to use your shower! There was another roach in mine!" I say, still dripping wet.

He is in the shower himself, so he yells out, "Ok, I'll be right out." Good thing there is no heat between us because this moment could have otherwise turned into a very spicy one since we are separated only by towels.

"Mimi, I think I'd like to attend a conference in Orlando tomorrow; you mind if I crash at your place tonight?" Torrance asks while he's drying off, out of my sight. I flash back to the last guy who stayed over at my house about a year ago. We got in an argument over cheese, and he left abruptly, leading my girls to get on me about having him at my house in the first place. I probably shouldn't let Torrance come over, but as he's looking at me now, waiting for an answer, I decide not to hold my baggage against him. He was a gentleman last night.

"Ok, you can follow me back to Orlando," I say.

"Cool, and hey, my friend gave me this great piece of halibut – maybe you can cook it for us?" Torrance asks.

This guy is asking for a lot – a place to stay and a meal. Goodness. But I guess it's better than Cheese, who didn't contribute anything to the meal we ultimately ended things over. "I suppose I can find a good recipe and pull something together," I respond.

We head back to Orlando and have another low-key evening together, in separate beds. But this time we have dinner and, thankfully, no roaches.

PREPARE FOR A BUMPY LANDING

Over the next week after Torrance returned to Philly, we continue our regular text communication. And then one night, Torrance gives me a call. "Hey... I have an opportunity to go to Cabo San Lucas for a couple of days of golf and networking Wednesday to Saturday. Any chance you can get away?" he asks.

"How did you know that I was just looking at an ad showing romantic getaways? It was highlighting this place called Eau Palm Beach, but Cabo sounds even better!" I say. "How did you get the opportunity?"

intuition
alarm #9

"The non-profit board I serve on is sponsoring the trip," he says. This sounds strange, but I suppose a sponsor could offer up free lodging to a non-profit 😳. I temper my excitement because Torrance has thrown out several trips at this point: Paris, another trip to Florida, and now Cabo.

I call Torrance a couple days later for an update on Cabo. "I'm starting to get the feeling you're going to Cabo without me? You haven't talked about it for the past few days, and the trip is next weekend, right?" I say.

"No, baby... I'm going to check it out... make sure you would be comfortable there and open the door for our return there together!" Torrance responds. He sure is good at spinning a negative into a positive.

What can I say? "Ok, good answer," I respond jokingly. "Will you activate your phone while you're in Mexico?"

"I hope to... but calls out will be costly, so please call me instead."

"Well, when you're on WiFi, you can call for free through FB Messenger," I say, "and Verizon has a very low-cost plan for Mexico. I'll send you the link. I used it last year when I went to the wedding I mentioned." We disconnect, and I bid Torrance safe travels.

A week later, I message Torrance to see if he made it to Cabo.

Me: How's it going?

Torrance: It's awesome here... All is going well!! This is at our villa outside of my room... Pool and jacuzzi.

Me: Nice. Yeah that's what I'm used to seeing in Cabo, rooms with their own pools that overlook the beach. It's on my list of places to go eventually. But the board sponsor didn't pay for all of that.

Torrance: Okay... I guess you know it all. Going to sleep. Have a great day!

Me: Sorry, I know I'm coming off like a B over text. We always get to this point.

Torrance doesn't respond for two days. I can tell from his passive-aggressive "you know it all" comment that he is in a mood. I decide to try and mend fences.

Me: I know you've been busy, but we haven't talked since Monday. Yes, I'm sure part of my baggage is at play, feeling suspicious that you are on this free luxury vacation and it's just you and your "board members."

Me: But it's also what we talked about before... Communication for me is like food or sex for you. I would've liked to have talked to you at some point over the last couple days. And it's just like the house in Sarasota. You send me photos and I'm confused bc I don't know what's going on or how you got there. And then you shut down bc you don't understand why I'm being difficult.

Torrance: If you don't know... then ask... Don't make statements. Clearly, I have access to free places... and clearly U have baggage... smh.

Me: You don't like for me to ask questions bc I come off like an investigator.

Me: You told me when last we left off you were going to "check it out so we could go back together" and then I see a pool. It's like, wait, how did that happen? It would've been easier had we talked bc over messenger it probably doesn't come off right.

Torrance: What are you complaining about now? We haven't talked since Monday... what?!? I told you I wasn't calling... I don't call from the US... and now you're complaining about Mexico?!? Jeez!

Me: And I told you calls are free thru this app.

Me: That's why I called you yesterday morning

Me: And left you a msg

Me: See the little phone above with the green light?

Me: Free on WiFi

Torrance: I am here checking out the resort, and I was sharing... Guess I shouldn't have. I will finish checking it out and fill you in when I get back...

Me: Don't worry about it. I think it's clear that my baggage will continue to keep us crippled, and your unwillingness to share general details like where you're staying and how you got it will always be a problem for me. I can't unpack my bags and you definitely don't want to give me what I need to do so. It's a cycle that we keep coming back to, and I think we'd be better off saving each other from future frustration.

my crazy #8

Me: This would've been an easier conversation via phone but since you don't want to call me, this is the best I can do. Would've called you again to leave this via voicemail but you would've said I was just calling to see if you were there with someone.

Torrance: Ok... smh ✌️

Me: Figured it'd be easier for you to bail than to help me feel safe and help my trust grow.

Me: And even if you cared, you wouldn't say it bc you don't want to give me the satisfaction of knowing you care

Me: It's just not healthy on either side

Torrance: It's 5am here... too much ado about nothing. How does your twisted baggage-riddled brain get that I'm unwilling to share general details when I'm sending U unsolicited pictures and reaching out to U!?!

Me: Lol it's not about the photos. It's about the how.

Torrance: I don't have time or patience for foolishness when I am trying. U didn't ask how... You made a statement, which annoyed me.

Me: The dots are never connected for me. It's just like Sarasota, you pop up with a house but didn't volunteer the fact that your friend is a member of the course, etc. It just leaves holes, and I'm a person who needs things to add up. I didn't ask you bc by me saying "the board didn't pay for that" I thought you would've voluntarily told me.

Me: And FYI, even better than photos is a FREE video call where I could've seen the whole place if you really wanted me to see it.

turn off #3

Torrance: I decided to let it go... and go to bed... but instead of realizing that perhaps you misspoke... you conjure up a bunch of bs... and now... you've gone and closed the door. So be it... Go hang out with your "friends" and have a great life!! I wish you nothing but the best!

Me: Lol and you totally don't mean a word of that. You were not going to bed and letting things go, you were sending sarcastic messages "have a great day!" They say don't go to sleep with a disagreement. I know this would've gone differently via phone but your stubbornness... which you don't own bc it's easier to blame everything on my baggage... won't allow you to give me what I needed, which was a simple conversation. So yes, I'm letting you out of your misery... You don't have to worry about calling me or catering to my needs. You can keep operating the way you have for 50 years and see if you end up with a different result in your next relationship.

Torrance: I have no reason to lie... if you could just give (the next brotha) the benefit of the doubt and keep all those ghosts out of that pretty lil head of yours... perhaps you can get out of your own way next time. I'm paying zero to stay here... but I (voluntarily) work my ass off as chair of the Finance Committee. Thanks to me... we just won a grant of $3M. This is a timeshare that the founder pays for anyway but only brings select folks to.

I never said I wouldn't answer if you called me... Moreover, U ass-umed that there was WiFi here and at

turn off #3

many places here... there is not. Since I hadn't been here b4, I wanted to manage your expectations. I WAS very tired and WAS going to let it go and go to bed. I'm just waking up now.

Torrance: U have some serious head issues Mimi... Perhaps that's why U are where you are relationship-wise! If I had a woman here... I could have made up a myriad of reasons why... or not... I am not married and we were not in an exclusive relationship. I DID want you to have a great day and I still do... why wouldn't I? Like

I told you before.... you are 254 and I always wanted us to be friends no matter what! I pray you find someone willing to deal with all your negative ass-umptions & conclusions based on old/tired info in your memory banks. U are a beautiful woman… inside and out... but a serious head case upstairs!! 😣

Me: Lol such kind words. I can tell how much you care. Was hoping you'd wake up in a better mood but so much for that

Me: Friends don't call each other names. We're both hurt and frustrated and I hate that this keeps happening.

Torrance: Well... to let you tell it like I wasn't going to sleep and let it go... Ms. Know-it-all... when nothing could have been further from the truth. I was trying to give you a pass and let it go... get some sleep, but noooo... U couldn't let it go... U had to keep digging yourself deeper and deeper into your own self-inflicted relationship coffin... for zero reason at all when U look back at this one day!

Me: Lol at relationship coffin. I'd rather be single than with someone who can't meet my basic needs. Communication is all I need and you're either not capable or simply unwilling to do so in a manner that will make me happy.

Torrance: Friends do call each other names... and friends do tell each other about themselves... but then again... you're probably an authority on that as well and only have friends that tell you wonderful things about yourself. Smh

Torrance: Well... I was trying to keep it 100 with you and give you some constructive criticism. Maybe you'll appreciate it one day. Ps... yes, I'm stubborn and set in my 50 years of ways to some degree... However, I was trying to work with you and be more flexible to how U like things. I woke up thinking about you (after a long day of meetings... golf... eating, drinking and smoking cigars) and attempted to communicate with you... too bad it wasn't good enough to make you happy. Smh 😞

Me: Lol. I need more transparency.

Torrance: Good luck with that! 👍

Me: Lol you're so kind. If you said you needed more from me, I wouldn't tell you that you had issues. I'd try to meet your expectations.

Me: Within reason.

Torrance: I did try...

Me: You tried to call me back?

Me: I left you a message yesterday morning. And I went to sleep last night and woke up this morning hoping to hear from you.

Me: Not bc I think you're there with someone. You invited me to come! But more just bc quality time is my love language and I just wanted to catch up with you and see how things were going. Plus, I mentioned I've had the roughest week at work and that's when I'd hope my friend would be there.

Torrance: No… but I told you I wasn't calling you from here... Why couldn't you just chillax or call me back?

Me: Lol bc you get mad when I call. And think I'm trying to pin you down or something. Trying to catch you in the act!

Torrance: Well... I'm in Mexico woman... juggling a million things with my son... court... tuition... my Mom... my job (up ALL night Tuesday)... this board retreat and having to deal with all your (stuff) on top of that... Jeez... I'm sorry

I didn't do enough for you... My advice: find some young local lad you can cougar... Uhhh, mentor and mold into what you require! Pow

I video call Torrance to put this ridiculous back-and-forth conversation to rest. Miraculously, we talk it through and return to our normal state – at least for the moment.

After getting back from Cabo in late August, Torrance starts talking about his next trip to Florida. "How about Labor Day Weekend?" Torrance asks.

"That could be cool. There's a music festival here in Orlando that weekend that my friends and I go to. Maybe you could join us?" I propose.

"Ok, well I have some business in Sarasota, but could maybe spend a few days in Orlando with you. Can you look at flights for me?" he asks.

"Uh, yeah, I can check schedules," I say, realizing the holiday is less than two weeks out. I send him a couple of screenshots of flights he could do, but he doesn't act quickly, just like before. As Labor Day approaches, he still hasn't booked anything.

A couple days later, I hear from him via text.

Torrance: Hey babe...

Me: Hi!

Torrance: Can you look into flights into Sarasota Thursday to Tuesday please?

Me: I'm actually about to drive home to get ready to host my friend Lisa and her mom in town from Philly tonight. I'm making dinner.

Even though he's talking to me like I'm his personal assistant, I still carve out time to call Torrance while I'm hosting dinner, but he doesn't answer. The next morning, he texts.

Torrance: Hope you had a great time with your friends... good morning.

Me: Morning! I'm about to get in the car for work. Did you find a flight?

Torrance: No... I didn't... I asked you to do that.

Torrance calls right away. "Hello?" I say with surprise, since he doesn't call often.

turn off #3

"Look, Mimi, you're flipping the script... You're not doing what I asked, Frugal Franny. You're not doing what you said you would do, and you're putting the ball of planning and paying for my flight into my court, which delays things considerably at best. Not cool... I've got a lot of work to do today, so I doubt I'll be able to look into anything today, and the way you turned that around really turns me off."

Wth? HAS THIS GUY LOST HIS MIND? He's on 10. I don't understand why he feels entitled to a free flight from me. *Let me try and speak rationally – I must be missing something.* "Torrance, when we discussed me getting your flight, I thought that *maybe* you wanted me to pay for it, but then I thought you just wanted me to look up options because you're always busy. At the time you asked a couple weeks ago, I figured that if you wanted my help paying, it wouldn't be so bad because it'd be a couple hundred dollars. But now it's closer to $400 because it's last-minute and it's Labor Day Weekend!" I say.

"Listen, Mimi, I have child support court fees, and my son's tuition is due. I don't need you making excuses and trying to find a way out of what we already discussed. Not cool..."

Wow. So not my problem, dude. "Torrance, I'm not trying to make excuses. It was never clear that you needed me to pay for your flight to Florida. If you're coming here for business, then you could book your flight using your credit card, and it'd be a tax-deductible business expense as opposed to me spending $400 out-of-pocket. Made sense to me as a means to save money, but somehow you must disagree."

"Don't worry about it... Keep your money and have a great weekend," Torrance says before hanging up on me.

It seems his fem voice was indicative of his personality all along. What a B.

Take a Page from My Book

There were plenty of times I Should've Left Torrance behind. For starters, I never should've resurrected him after seven years. I should've known that if he was worth my time, I would've kept in touch with him.

He raised his voice and lost his temper one too many times, especially when we were so early into getting to know one another, and his points were never valid. Petty frequent arguments early on are a bad sign. I Should've Left When he lost his temper in Cabo, among other times. But getting mad at me for not paying for your flight? Uh, you gotta go. ✌️

Book of 57

♡

57

THE INITIAL ENCOUNTER

It's early September, and election season is heating up. I'm on my way to a political fundraiser on a random Tuesday night. I'm so not feeling it after a long workday, but my friend Olivia asks me to go in her place, and I just can't say no. Plus, I do love to meet new people and support my friends – not to mention that my man-slate is completely clean after Torrance "flew" off the handle a few weeks ago, getting mad at me for not paying for his flight.

Approaching the political fundraiser at Pointe Orlando, a popular entertainment complex, I cross paths with a tall, distinguished-looking gentleman. He's attractive and wearing a full dark suit, a nice tie, and a pair of dark-rimmed glasses. He stands out to me because he is very well-dressed for such a touristy area. I assume he's heading to the political fundraiser as well.

I somewhat greet him with my eyes, but because he's on his phone, I continue walking to the fundraiser, and he stays a few steps behind me. As I walk into the casual, Southern-themed BB King's restaurant, the suited gentleman hangs back outside, still on the phone. Once inside, I'm immediately greeted by Carl, the political candidate for commissioner and the fundraiser's host. Carl gives me a rundown of how the evening will go: live jazz, food, drinks, cameras recording the event, etc. – not your average stuffy fundraiser. And while Carl and I are mid-conversation, the distinguished gentleman from outside walks up to us.

"Hey, Holden, it's good to see you, man!" Carl says as he hugs his friend. "Oh, and allow me to introduce you to Mimi – she's a friend of Olivia's. Mimi came out to support tonight since Olivia couldn't make it."

Holden – looking even better up close at about 6'2" and very clean-cut – extends his hand to me. "It's a pleasure to meet you, Mimi – a friend of Olivia's is a friend of ours," says Holden.

turn on #2

I smile as Carl and Holden exchange pleasantries, and then the three of us engage in brief small talk. Carl has to break away to tend to his other guests, leaving Holden and I alone. "Mimi, can I get you a drink?" Holden asks.

"Oh, that is so kind, but no, thank you," I respond as I survey the small and boring-looking crowd, thinking to myself, *I won't be here long*. But, on second thought, I realize that if I am going to endure this somewhat strange event for any length of time, I might need a crutch. "You know what, Holden? I will take you up on your offer if you don't mind," I say. Being every part the gentleman that he appears to be, Holden immediately turns toward the bar, which is just steps away, and proceeds to order a Sauvignon Blanc at my request.

turn on #1

Thanking Holden, with wine in hand, I turn to look for a seat when I hear Holden's voice. "Where would you like to sit?" *Interesting*. I was not ex-pecting to have company, but at the same time, I'm relieved Holden is asking to join me; I don't know a soul at this fundraiser.

"Hmm, perhaps over there?" I say, pointing to a mostly empty table against the window, near the stage.

"That looks good – I'll follow you," Holden replies, and so the evening begins. I think Holden is just being nice to me because I don't know anyone at the event and because I'm Olivia's friend.

I also think he's being nice to me because, as I learned during our initial conversation, Holden is best friends and business partners with the candidate, Carl – they share a consulting practice in town. But shortly after we take our seats, I realize Holden might have more in mind than just being a simple fundraiser conversation partner. Holden sits rather close to me, and I get the feeling he isn't keeping me company for Olivia and Carl's sake. He is interested in something more. Before I know it, Holden's arm is on the back of my chair – kind of like your high-school boyfriend did at the movie theater with the yawn and open-arm stretch move. Holden has me locked in with the window at my back, him to my right, the table in front of me, and now his arm wrapped around my chair to my left. *Well, alright, then.*

Holden proceeds to engage only me as we generally ignore the other couple of people at our table and try to talk over the program, which features the boisterous candidate, Commissioner Carl, on the mic. "We have an exciting evening ahead for you. On sax tonight, we have Mr. Jim Whitfield." The small audience applauds as Carl continues to explain the flow of the evening.

Meanwhile, Holden and I are having a full side-conversation which is starting to mirror a first date. "So, where are you from?" Holden asks.

"I'm originally from Philadelphia, but I've been in Orlando for over 10 years," I respond, taking a sip of wine from my almost-empty glass. Holden shares that he is from Palm Beach County. "Oh, I love The Breakers but have always wanted to check out the Eau Resort there – have you been?" I ask.

"Of course I have – you would really love it there," Holden responds, before adding, "We should go sometime."

Well, that does it. As if his arm resting on the back of my chair and undivided attention didn't say enough, it is now official:

Holden wants a little more than a fundraiser companion. What Holden doesn't know is that I'm already attracted to him, and by  the offer of a trip, he opens me up like a daffodil in springtime. I LOVE a man with a plan – tell me where you're taking me, and if it meets my standards, you've got my attention. I bottle my enthusiasm, though, as to not look antsy, especially given that I've only known this man for about 35 minutes and, realistically, the chances of us ever going on a trip together are pretty slim (not to mention all of the broken trip promises that pay-for-my-flight Torrance made over the last few months). "We'll have to see if we can make that happen," I respond.

turn on #5

We continue our rather intimate side-conversation, much to candidate Carl's frustration. He keeps giving us dirty looks for talking during his event – especially since cameras are rolling. But at this point, my interest is piqued from the picture Holden has painted of us at a fabulous beach resort, and I couldn't care less about Carl and his boring fundraiser – he's lucky I'm even here.

Holden and I are talking about our respective careers – his as an investigator and mine as an auditor – when the waitress approaches our table. "Can I get you both a refill?" Holden looks at me and I agree to take part in round two since the conversation is just getting interesting, and I am all in at this point.

After the waitress steps away to the bar, I turn to Holden, double-checking his ringless left-hand, and I ask, "So, have you been married?"

"I'm actually going through a divorce right now," he responds, and somehow the combination of his tone and body language translates as "disappointed yet relieved" – which I think is the feeling of most divorcees.

"How long were you married?" I ask.

"Thirty years," Holden replies as he takes a sip of his scotch.

Wow. While such a long marriage can say a lot about a person (committed, patient, etc.), it is a bit of a barrier – what can I do with someone just out of a 30-year marriage? Well, besides the obvious – which is not me. "Wow, that is certainly a long time – you had children together?"

"Yes, in fact, we had four children – all of whom are in college and beyond now."

Whoa, four children can make a dent in one's pocket (sorry, that's where my mind goes). But Holden gives off an air of financial security and confidence, which I find very attractive. "Wow, that's great! What an accomplishment," I reply, trying not to let on how hard his personal situation hit me. Thankfully, the soothing live jazz playing in the background, the second round of drinks, and the thought of a potential beach weekend getaway make the tough conversation about Holden's personal life a little less painful.

My curiosity leads me to ask Holden why his marriage ended – especially after 30 years. I'm surprised how candid he is. He explains to me that his wife had cheated with someone they knew – someone who lived in their neighborhood – crazy. He gives details about how she would say she was working late (she is a nurse) and how he ultimately found out through a friend that she was sleeping with their neighbor. He even added that his kids found out about the affair and, therefore, have a better relationship with him than with their mom.

I know I shouldn't think this way, but I always have trouble believing the whole "wife cheated" story – maybe because my girlfriends do not cheat, while I've had several cheating boyfriends. I fully recognize I'm a bit biased because of my cheating exes. However, I also think that the "woe is me, she did me wrong" approach is an easy way for a guy to gain sympathy

intuition
alarm #10

from a woman. It brings out the nurturing (and maybe also the vindictive) side of a woman. From my brief encounter with Holden, I somewhat believe he could be the innocent victim of a cheating wife, but I do have one eyebrow raised...

Despite the four kids, the cheating wife drama, and the fact that he looks a lot older than the men I usually go for, I really enjoy talking to Holden because he seems so successful and intelligent. I'm a self-proclaimed sapiosexual, so his intelligence and his confidence are what lead me to feel the chemistry between us and keep me here for the full fundraiser.

turn on #1

As the event winds down at around 7:30, Holden leans in and asks me, "Would you like to go somewhere nearby for a bite to eat?"

I'm really enjoying the conversation and it is still early so, I respond, "Sure, why not?" We say our goodbyes and head back outside into Pointe Orlando – one of the city's prime restaurant and nightclub areas – though I don't expect it to be especially lively on a Tuesday night.

"Where would you like to go?" Holden asks.

"Hmmm... How about Tommy Bahama – we can sit at the bar?" I respond. I had eaten there recently and remember that the guacamole and the grilled chicken skewers were awesome.

We enter Tommy Bahama's bar area, where Holden pulls out my barstool. "Can I have a scotch on the rocks?" Holden says to the bartender, "and would you like the same wine, Mimi?"

"Yes," I respond. We order drinks, a few apps, and we continue our conversation. "So, where did you go to school, Holden?"

"Ah, I attended Florida State as an undergrad and the University of Alabama for grad school."

Nice, I think to myself. I love a well-educated man. He goes on to explain that he moved to Orlando after grad school in the early 80s and became a private investigator, later starting his own practice. "Tell me about your kids," I suggest.

"Three of my kids are in college, and it is so expensive. I pay all of their tuition: upwards of $60K per year."

Wow, I think to myself as I take a bite of the yummy chicken skewers. "So, any upcoming travels for you, Holden?" I ask after sharing that I am heading to London and Dublin in a few days.

"Well, I usually take one big trip per year to Toronto for Caribana," he says. "I've gone every year for the past 30 years. I love the Caribbean culture and music."

Hmmm, fascinating, I think – especially when he shares that he goes without his wife. I have attended a couple of Caribbean Carnival events with my friend Rachel. I know how wild some of the parties can be, so I'm getting a somewhat different picture in my head of the suited-up Holden seated before me with his studious glasses, as being anything but conservative. I'm also thinking about the hefty expense involved – he references spending about $7K annually on the Carnival trip. Unreal. "And I know I shouldn't ask this, but how old are you, Holden?"

"I'm 57," he responds. I do a quick calculation in my head; he is 19 years my senior. Holden did say he started work in the early 80s, so his age makes sense – I guess I just don't want to believe it.

I try not to look like I'm taken aback when I share, "Oh, I see. Well, I'm 38."

"Well, that's perfect!" Holden says, and I feel like he is licking his lips in excitement.

Slow down, old man.

As the conversation continues, I start to realize that, in addition to Holden being a bit old for me, he has a LOT going on in his life, so

I tell him I could see us being friends for now – especially given that he is still going through the divorce process of his 30-year marriage. I imagine he'll feel being friends will be ideal for him now, and after all, I do call myself the divorcee whisperer, as I'm known to help re-acquaint people with the Orlando social scene ☺.

Holden disagrees with his placement in the friend zone, but we exchange numbers nevertheless, and he walks me to my car. "Can I give you a call tomorrow?" he asks after I open my car door. I've established rules for things a guy must do upon meeting me in order for things to progress – offer me a drink, be friendly to my friends, and make sure I get home ok. Though I have drawn the friendship line with Holden, if there is a chance for anything more down the line, he needs to meet my basic criteria.

While I'd have preferred Holden to organically decide to check on me, I figure I can provide a little nudge. "You're not going to make sure I get home ok tonight?" I ask.

Holden smiles with a tinge of "Why didn't I think of that?" disappointment and replies, "Of course, I'll call you tonight, Mimi."

I am somewhat hoping that Holden calls on my way home because even though I have placed him in the friend zone, I still enjoyed getting to know him. Instead, I call my mom to confess that I met someone who is only about 10 years younger than her, and she replies, "Whew hew!" Lol. Mommy, for whatever reason, has NO problem with me giving the old-timers play. Now that I'm getting older, I'm definitely pulling more men with AARP benies.

As I'm getting ready for bed at home and still recapping the night with my Mom, Holden calls. "Oh, Mom, that's my other line... It's Holden," I say, smiling to myself.

"Oh! Well, let me let you go!" she says with exuberance, forgetting I told her that Holden and I are not altar-bound.

"Hey, Holden," I say as I click over. "Did you get home safely?"

"Yes, I did, Mimi. Thank you for a great evening. You really made my night," Holden responds. I smile, and I thank him for the evening which I really did enjoy. "So, do you think you'll have time to go out with me before your trip to London this weekend?" Holden asks.

Immediately, I respond, "Yes, that'd be great," though in my head, I know I have a lot to do to get ready for my trip. I enjoyed our exchange so much that I'm definitely willing to squeeze in time with him this week.

As it turns out, much to my surprise, a couple days pass before I hear from Holden again. Even worse, when he finally reaches out, it's via text – no call.

Holden: I hope you are excited about your upcoming trip. Have a great time and take photos to preserve those memories. You are a really cool lady.

What? He said nothing about going out on the date he had previously requested. So, I text back.

Me: Hey stranger, thought you wanted to catch up before I left but guess you got tied up.

Holden: Oh, I got tied up trying to complete a statement for a client case.

caution #8

Hmmm, ok. I don't like that Holden didn't keep his word, and it is a definite red flag that I had to prompt him to acknowledge that he asked for my time but then didn't follow through. I put Holden out of my mind and proceed to have fun and meet new men on a girls' trip to London and Dublin (although the overseas men don't act right, either. Sheesh!)

After flying back from the trip, I wake up Sunday morning feeling surprisingly refreshed (thank you, Norwegian airlines). I find myself wanting to go out on a date, which is not normal for me. Maybe I want to continue the excitement from the European

my crazy #8

caution #9

adventure, or maybe I just want to go out with Holden again, but whatever the case, I'm thinking about him and wishing he'd call. So, I decide to take matters into my own hands and call him myself. What happens? His phone goes right to voicemail. *Hmm, maybe he was dialing someone at the same time I called.* I call again about a minute later, and it's the same thing – right to voicemail. Oh, and his voicemail is full – red flag numero deux. It's about 11:00 a.m. on a Sunday, so I think that maybe he's in church. I text him instead.

Me: Hey there. I made it back home safely. I hope all is well.

I don't hear back from Holden until 24 hours later, when he texts back Monday morning.

Holden: I'm glad you had a safe trip. I'll call you later tonight.

I am definitely disappointed it took Holden a full day to get back to me after my Sunday morning outreach, but I'm glad to finally hear from him. However, all hopes are dashed when Monday night comes and goes with no call from Holden.

MOVING ON – MAYBE...

At this point, Holden is completely off my dating bench after failing to call and having previously flaked on his requested meet-up. I suddenly feel the need to go on a "man-cleanse" – my own made-up term for clearing the bench. It is a natural, knee-jerk reaction to another man let-down. After the year I've had with men – from discovering that the man I was about to introduce to my parents as my boyfriend was married with a child (Vegas), to having another guy who was at least going to be a friend become overly aggressive with me (Aruba Luke), to getting yelled at for not paying for a flight, (Torrance), to having a guy I met last week at a Dublin nightclub stick his hand down the back of my pants and grope me – it's time for a purge. I need to press the reset button and get away from men.

Luckily for me, I have a girls' beach weekend planned just a couple days after Holden disappears – the getaway is going to be the welcomed distraction I need. Though our annual Siesta Key Beach trip is tainted with the stench of dead fish from "the red tide" (an apparent environmental phenomenon that kills thousands of fish, sending them to shore), I don't know the last time I've felt so free and happy. I laugh so hard one night as my friend Leila and I dance like silly teenage girls in our hotel suite; I knew I needed this trip. Pretty much every day of my adult life I've been dating someone, and this is the first time I can recall being man-free and just feeling like no one has an influence over my state of happiness – I can just be at peace.

In the weeks after Holden disappears, I gain some clarity on who I am and what I will and will not accept. I know I often fall into relationships ignoring up-front red-flags, and I stay too long because I don't want to hurt the other person by denying their advances. But I really feel like I've recently had an epiphany and vow to take control – I vow not to compromise my happiness for anyone else's sake. I also realize how to be truly at peace being 100% single and surrounding myself with family and friends. I know I can stay in this "party of one" state, happily ever after, if the single life is the best path for me.

But, as fate would have it, Holden and I cross paths again, almost like we did the night we met at Pointe Orlando walking from the parking garage. This time it is even more serendipitous. I get an unexpected text from my friend Angie.

Angie: Hey Mimi, are you open to having coffee with Holden Williams? [She includes a photo.] He is an investigator in Orlando. Just met him at a party in Miami… very successful, has his own consulting firm!

intuition
alarm #8

I laugh out loud. *Only me.* Funny thing, Holden doesn't look nearly as attractive (and actually looks pretty shady) in the picture she sent as he does in person. Maybe I'm projecting his shady disappearing act onto his picture, or maybe I'm seeing his true colors for the first time since his distinguished gentleman appearance isn't standing in front of me.

Me: Omg, I just went out with him a month ago, Ang.

Gosh, that sounds bad – my friend Angie meets a guy randomly in a bar, in another city, and I've already practically dated him. What are the chances?

Me: Remember I told you about the guy 57 I met at Pointe Orlando last month?

Angie: OMG! Hilarious. I thought he looked familiar. Okay, scratch that thought then!

Me: LOL, it's all good. Tell him he missed out.

A few hours later, at 2:00 a.m., guess who calls? Holden – but I'm asleep. He doesn't leave a voicemail, but he leaves a text message.

Holden: Mimi, I know that something is meant for us. I met this beautiful woman tonight that knew you. I told her that you are so beautiful that you frightened me.

I wake up several hours later, read Holden's message, and roll my eyes – it sounds like complete BS.

Me: Haaaaaa! I know that was alcohol talking at 2am or Angie told you to say that.

Holden: Mimi, it's a small world.

Me: Yup, you can run but you can't hide.

Holden: I don't want to run. You will see.

Me: Mmm hmmm... You're assuming I'd give you another chance after you broke 2 basic promises.

Holden: You owe me at least one dinner.

Me: That's debatable.

A week goes by, and I have put Holden far out of my mind – again. My man-cleanse is working well. I have no desire to go out with him or anyone else – it's time to just focus on me. However, nine days after Holden's chance meeting with Angie, he pops up again when he texts me.

Holden: I would like to have dinner with you one night this week. Let me know when you are available.

I take about 40 minutes before responding. I'm torn. There is something about this man that still intrigues me, but I already

my crazy #8

know he's bad news and doesn't deserve my time. But then, I remember I need a date for a dinner party Saturday, and he would fit the bill. Plus, it will allow me to take control of where the evening will go.

Me: Funny, you must've known I have a dinner party to attend this Saturday and was trying to think who to invite. Are you free Saturday at 7pm? It's casual.

Holden: I have my daughter in town, but I can take three hours, I really want that time with you.

His chance meeting with Angie, and perhaps her probing him as to why we didn't work out as a couple, might have given him new energy to somewhat pursue me again. I can't deny that he has opened me back up to the possibilities. I just hope curiosity won't kill the cat (i.e., me).

Holden offers to pick me up for our Saturday night dinner. While that would've been delightful, I have an earlier commitment which puts me close to the dinner party. So, we agree to meet at the dinner location.

Holden calls upon arrival. "Mimi, uh, I think I'm here, but what is this place? Are you trying to set me up or kill me?"

I laugh. "Oh, my goodness, no. I haven't been to the location before. What do you see?" I ask. As Holden describes the warehouse building in front of him, which his GPS had taken him to, I recall attending another event at the same wine distillery, and then it clicks. "Ah, I think you're actually in the right place," I say.

I pull up about 20 minutes later – Holden was early for the event – and by the time I arrive, he explains that well-dressed people had entered the warehouse distillery, so he has gained comfort that I am not going to ax him once we're inside ☺.

Holden steps out of his black BMW SUV to greet me at my car. "Mimi, it's so good to see you," he says as he hugs me. I have to give it to him, he is well-dressed once again, in a nice gray suit with a tie. All previous frustrations with him have melted away during my cleanse period, and since I have no expectations anymore, I'm looking forward to a nice evening.

Holden guides me through the dark gravel parking lot and up to the warehouse door. "Mimi, come in! I'm so glad you could make it," says my friend Tricia, who is hosting the dinner to promote her new restaurant.

"Oh, thank you so much for inviting me, Tricia. This looks great," I say as I look around the lobby area remembering the event I had attended there previously.

"Tricia, I'd like you to meet Holden," I say, motioning her to welcome my evening date.

"Hello, Tricia. It's nice to meet you," he responds, extending his hand to hers. I definitely think Holden and I look good together. And because my friend Tricia is in her 50s, like Holden, I feel I picked the perfect date to mesh with her party attendees.

"Mimi, we have a full three-course meal planned for tonight; you're going to love it. Just head down the hall and to the left where we're having cocktails before we start dinner," Tricia explains.

"Thanks so much, Tricia. We're looking forward to it!"

Holden leads me down the hall to the cocktail area Tricia had described. We find a pretty diverse group of people seated around a big, dark oak wooden bar. In the background are barrels upon barrels of wine, stacked Costco-style on huge shelves up to the warehouse ceiling. It is definitely a unique setting, but it's pretty cool.

Looking around, the only person I recognize is Tricia's mother-in-law, so I suggest that Holden and I go over to greet her. "Hello, Mrs. Pickard. How are you," I say as I turn toward my date. "Oh, and this is Holden." He almost looks presidential among the people in the room.

Holden extends his hand. "It's a pleasure to meet you."

Mrs. Pickard seems to stare at him, almost like she wanted to take him home. "Gosh, you look familiar," she says.

"Well, I do private investigation work," Holden explains with confidence.

Mrs. Pickard laughs. "Well, hopefully I don't know you then." We all laugh in unison. Holden has a certain presence that commands attention and respect.

turn on #11

Holden and I continue to make our way around the bar, passing an older couple seated nearby. Unexpectedly, Holden extends his hand to the unfamiliar couple. "Hello, I'm Holden, and this is Mimi," he says. *Wow, impressive.* He just took over as if he's the invitee and I'm his date – it's an instant turn-on.

"Hello, it's nice to meet you," I say as I extend my hand while still absorbing Holden's ability to take over the reins. I guess this is one of the benefits of dating a grown man; I don't need to be in control 😊.

We meet several other couples during the cocktail hour, we tour the distillery and toast plentiful glasses of wine with the owner. Through every step, Holden continues to impress me with his social skills and charisma – he is very liked by the diverse crowd.

Tricia gathers everyone for dinner around a huge 40-person table. "Wow, this is really awesome, Mimi. Thanks so much for inviting me," Holden says. I can tell that Holden is genuinely having a nice time – and so am I. We take our seats for dinner, and we end up sitting next to people who pretty much keep to themselves. So, Holden and I end up just engaging with each other – almost like

turn off #4

the night we met at the political fundraiser. The DJ is playing some great 70s soul music – Kool and the Gang's "Summer Madness" to be exact – and I can't help but get into it. Meanwhile, Holden doesn't move a finger. It may sound crazy, but music is my thing. It stirs my soul, and I love to share that with someone.

"I listen to Soca music every day," Holden responds when I question him on why he's not into the music. I think to myself, *Shoot me now.* (Apologies to my Caribbean friends 😊.) I recently took a trip to Miami Carnival and know that daily Soca music is just not for me.

"So, Mimi, I told Carl that I didn't keep in contact with you because you scared me," Holden says, cutting into the caprese in front of him.

"Is that so?" I remark, somewhat sarcastically, turning to see his face as he speaks.

"Yes, I told Carl that if you and I dated, I could see us married in a few years, and I'm just not sure I'm ready for that right now."

I almost choke on my mozzarella. *Wow... Really?* Then, I think to myself, *Well, I am a good catch, so maybe he is really nervous about what could or couldn't happen with us.*

Holden goes on. "And when you told me you only wanted to be friends, I knew I wanted more, so I figured it was best to just avoid you."

I'm looking Holden straight in the eye now, trying to assess how honest he's being, but I can't call it. *Is he really smitten with me and looking for something more? Or is he just looking for a "friends with benefits" arrangement and trying to bait me with marriage talk?* "Well, Holden, I don't know... Maybe I jumped the gun. Maybe there is something here," I respond as he pours me another glass of Pinot Noir to pair with my grilled snapper.

I'm not sure. Maybe it's the wine talking, coupled with seeing Holden in action tonight, engaging perfect strangers so effortlessly, but despite his prior disappearances and let-downs, I'm no longer completely determined to keep him in the friend zone. However, in my confused state, I figure it's best to change the subject because I sincerely have no answers for what to do about us right now. "So, from here, I'm heading to a party at Phil Patrick's house," I say.

Holden's eyes light up "Oh?" he says, to which I reply, "You're welcome to join me if you want."

"Oh, Phil, wow. I'd love to see him!" Holden says with excitement. He had mentioned knowing Phil when we first met, and I purposefully didn't mention going to Phil's party earlier in the evening because I wanted to see how things would go. But as the dinner party is winding down, I feel like I don't want our time together to end just yet, so I'm happy Holden accepts the invitation to join me.

"Perfect. Let's get ready to head out," I tell Holden. Holden and I say our goodbyes to Tricia, Mrs. Pickard, and the interesting group of people we met. We head back out to the dark gravel parking lot.

Holden turns to me as we near my car door. "Mimi, I really had a great time with you this evening," he says in a somewhat flirtatious tone. He wraps his arms around me and pulls me in for a hug.

"So did I, Holden, you made a great date," I say smiling and feeling his embrace.

Holding me close, Holden looks down in my eyes and says, "I don't want to let you go," as he squeezes me tighter.

"Mmm," I moan while the pitch-dark parking lot and Pinot Noir are working their magic on me. "I think we should get going, Holden," I say looking back up into his eyes. Holden just squeezes me even tighter as I feel his hand drop down my back, below my waist, gripping my bottom while he thrusts his hips toward me, allowing me to feel his *excitement*. Then, Holden tries to lean in to kiss my lips, but I turn to give him my cheek. As turned on as I am, I know he hasn't earned a kiss. My avoidance breaks the somewhat steamy moment.

"Ok," Holden says, "I guess we should get going." I can't deny that I'm all-the-way turned-on at this point. If not for his prior misgivings, I might've been tempted to do something crazy in that parking lot (I think I can fit in the back of an SUV). But at this point in my life, I'm trying to exercise more restraint and invoke my inner angel ☺. No need to get membership in the "mile-low club." (not to mention again that this man has not yet demonstrated that he deserves me).

Holden's phone goes off as we separate from one another and try to bring down the heat between us. "Sh*t, that's my daughter," he remarks somewhat angrily.

"Oh, do you need to grab the call?" I ask, somewhat puzzled by his tone.

turn off #11

"No, I'm not speaking to her right now. That b***h was supposed to come down here last night – I paid for her and her no-good-husband's flight from New York, but they decided not to come and didn't tell me."

Wow. Wow. Wow. Did this fool just call his own daughter the B-word? Wth?! I'm shocked. The seemingly distinguished gentleman is anything but. I can't imagine my father EVER calling me out of my name, and definitely not a B! Unbelievable. "How could you say that about your daughter?" I ask. "I get that you're upset with her for wasting your money on an unused plane ticket, but the B-word?" I add.

"You're right, I'm sorry. She just really makes me upset, especially that good-for-nothing husband of hers always taking advantage," he responds with a slightly more mellow tone. Well, this was a conversation that we certainly couldn't continue in the dark warehouse parking lot. I try to put it out of my mind, but I know in the back of my mind that he just put the final nail in his coffin. *If you can call your daughter a B, then what the h*ll will you call me one day?*

Being confrontational is just not in my nature. While some may say I should've sent Holden packing seconds after calling his

my crazy #6

daughter a B, I just can't do it. Plus, as bad as it may sound, I am still turned on from our close encounter in the parking lot. At least now I'm conscious of my bad decisions and know I will remain in control. "You can follow me. Phil's house is only about 10 minutes away," I say to Holden through my car window as we drive off.

On the way to Phil's house, we stop by the liquor store for a gift – it is Phil's birthday after all. "How about this bottle"? Holden asks holding up a big bottle of dark liquor. I walk over to him to take a look. I don't know a thing about dark liquor, but I know the price tag says $109, and I have to swallow my inner cheap girl.

"Umm, sure, if you think that's best... I take it that's what you like to drink?" I ask.

"Yes, this is my favorite, and I'm sure Phil will love it," Holden responds. *Well, that's refreshing* – he might call his daughter a B but cares enough to buy an old friend an expensive bottle of scotch. I'm not quite sure how this all stacks up, but at this point, I'm just going with the flow.

Holden and I jump back in our cars and complete the five-minute trip to Phil's house. "Mimi, is that you?" Phil yells from his driveway, looking through my rolled-down car window.

"Yes, Phil, it's your favorite person, back to help you celebrate your birthday for the second night in a row!" (I had attended Phil's grander birthday party the night before. Holden was supposed to attend too, but he mentioned during dinner that he decided to stay home because he was upset about his daughter not flying in.) After dinner, of course, I learned just how upset he was with "that B." Smh.

"Oh, great, Mimi. I'm so glad you could make it. Who is that pulling in behind you?" Phil asks with a puzzled look on his face as he eyes the unfamiliar black SUV in front of his house.

"Well, Phil, I brought you a little surprise," I say as I get out of my car. Holden steps out of his car, into yet another dark area, and heads over towards Phil.

"Holden, man, is that you!?!" Phil asks excitedly.

"Yeah, man, it's me!" Holden says as he and Phil go to hug one another like long-lost brothers. *Well, this is working out nicely*, I think to myself. Phil seems genuinely happy to reconnect with his friend of 20 years who he hasn't seen in over 10 years. Phil, Holden and I walk into Phil's house, and to my disappointment, there are only about five people here – it's now after 10:00, so I definitely thought there'd be more people by this point.

"I'm so sorry. I thought there would be more people," I whisper to Holden as we enter the kitchen behind Phil. Holden motions with his hands that he is fine and for me not to worry.

"Hey, guys, make yourselves at home. There's plenty of food and drinks," Phil says as he points over to the bar and kitchen. Holden and I make ourselves comfortable as we stand between the kitchen and the living room, which had been cleared to be used as a dance-floor.

"Well, we don't have to stay long," I say softly to Holden.

"Oh, it's fine. I'm enjoying the music," he says while taking a sip of the expensive scotch he brought for Phil. Phil is from the  Caribbean, and so Holden's favorite music is play-ing. "You know, Mimi, I just love listening to Soca, sitting on my patio, and smoking a cigar," Holden says, doing a little two-step to the music and feel-ing lively.

turn off #4

Trying to hide my dismay, I say, "Oh? Cigars? How often do you smoke?"

"As often as I can – it really relaxes me, and with everything I have going on, I really need it," he responds.

Well, this night can't get much worse, I think to myself as we tran-sition to the nearby couch. I know cigars are quite popular among elite men like Holden, but it's one thing to have a cigar out from time to time with friends and another thing to have a cigar at home regularly. Nightly smoking on the patio is just not for me. "Oh, I see," I say, trying not to let him see that any chances of him kissing me on the couch just went up in "smoke."

"Yeah, on any Friday night, you can find me with my cigar, Soca music, and my dog on the patio unwinding," Holden says.

turn off #4

He couldn't have painted a more dreadful picture for me – first cigars, and now a dog, too? "A dog? What kind of dog do you have?" Once I ask, I realize I don't know why I did – it doesn't matter since I don't know ish about dogs and I wouldn't be comfortable dating virtually anyone with any kind of dog since they just aren't my thing.

"I have a golden retriever," Holden says, "but I have to share the dog with my ex, so I only have him every other week," he adds sadly. "It's funny, though – I haven't had that dog in a week, but his hair is still all over my house. That dog sheds so much!" Holden shares lovingly.

I can't control my eyes from widening. *Can this man get any worse for me?* He has a B for a daughter, and now I have to worry about this other B shedding dog hair all over the house, while his cigar smoke fills the air, and he doesn't seem to care... *Omg, check, please!* "Oh, wow, Holden. You must really love dogs. I'm actually allergic to many breeds, especially those that shed," I share.

"Yes, I've had a dog since I was a kid," Holden says, "and I used to keep them outside until I realized how the barking can bother the neighbors and most HOAs nowadays don't allow it, so now my dog is usually in my bed, and I love it." Not that anything is salvageable at this point, but any glimmer of hope for Holden and I walking hand-in-hand at the Eau Palm Beach Resort is dashed the moment I envision his hairy dog rolling around on his bed. I decide to change the subject since prying this man away from his hairy dog is a lost cause. I figure I'll see if Holden and I are at least aligned on one other key factor – religion (reflecting on how things went earlier this year with Luke).

"So, do you attend church, Holden?" I ask, looking out to the dance area which, in the blink of an eye, has a few partiers that came in while I was engrossed in conversation with Holden.

"I do attend church. I'm Lutheran. I'll be there tomorrow morning at 10:00 a.m.!" he says proudly.

"Wow, that's impressive. So, you attend regularly?" I ask, for clarity.

"I don't miss a Sunday," says Holden.

"Gotcha. Well, I would've killed to meet a church-going man like you some time ago (well, not killed, but you know what I mean), but I no longer practice a specific religion and prefer to be aligned with my mate on faith," I say. After I explain this to Holden, he basically responds, "So what?" but I've been down this path before with Luke, and I know it just does not work for me. Not to mention, this is round-hole-square-peg issue number five (or more) at this point.

"Well, it's getting late and we both have long drives. I guess it's time to head home?" I say, looking at Holden and feeling like all sparks have been officially extinguished. Holden's arm is around me, as we have been cuddled up on Phil's couch looking like two high-school lovers, but in my mind, we are anything but.

"I could keep holding you all night, Mimi," he says as he pulls me in closer. I keep my head and body facing straight ahead on the couch like I'm mummified. I probably had a half barrel of wine tonight, and I know it's easy for me to have a weak moment, but there is no way I'm making out with this man on my friend's couch with onlookers around – not to mention the, like, 15 strikes against him at this point.

Holden tries to kiss me, and I give him my cheek once again. "You know, Holden, I like you, but I'm really thinking that we truly are better as friends," I tell him. I don't look his way but pat him on the thigh to ease any pain from my words.

"Well, it's up to you, Mimi... It's up to you," says Holden. He takes the final sip of his over-priced scotch, and we get up from the couch.

Phew! I dodged that awkward situation and stayed true to my inner angel ☺. "Holden, I'm going to say goodbye to Phil, hit the restroom, and I'll meet you outside," I say.

"Ok," Holden responds as he walks his empty glass into the kitchen. Minutes later, after saying goodbye to Phil and a couple others, I walk outside to find Holden standing just by the door. There is a tall woman standing there with him, facing him. They are engaged in conversation. I hear laughter as I approach the two of them.

I extend my hand to the beautiful woman. "Hi, I'm Mimi. I saw you inside, but we didn't get to meet," I say kindly, taking my place to the left of Holden.

"Oh, nice to meet you, Mimi. I'm Claire," she says. I can't explain it, but there is a feeling I have walking up to the two of them talking, almost like I'm interrupting them. They couldn't have been talking for more than five minutes, but they seemed engaged. And they can't possibly know one another because they hadn't spoken inside. I have to get a clearer picture of what is going on. "So, do you two know each other?" I ask, looking up to Holden on my right.

"Oh, I was just outside here waiting for you when Claire walked out, and we started talking," Holden responds.

"Oh, ok," I say. I couldn't help but notice Claire's voice when she introduced herself to me – on top of being tall and gorgeous, she has the most melodious voice, and so I have to ask, "Claire, are you a singer by chance?"

"Actually, yes, I am. I sing for the Orlando Opera, and I moved here because I initially sang for Disney. I used to play the role of Pocahontas," she responds.

Well, goodness, is this girl not perfect? Sheesh. "Oh, wow," I exclaim, looking to Holden to see his reaction, which appears to be impressed like mine. I really feel like she must have an interest in Holden, given that her eyes are still fixated on him and neither of them is moving – in fact, they are blocking the way to the cars. I figure I'll break the awkwardness. "That's so impressive, Claire, goodness. So, what kind of music do you like?" I ask.

"Actually," Claire responds, "although I'm from Connecticut, I have a fascination with Caribbean music."

Well, that does it – have I just met Holden's twin or something? "How about Soca?" I ask, for clarification.

"Yes, I love Soca music!" Claire says with exuberance, still not giving any indication whether she is going to step away and allow us to leave. So, at this point, I'm thinking this girl is perfect for him, but there's one more test. "So, Claire, this will seem like an odd question, but are you a dog person?"

Claire's eyes light up with glee. "Oh, I love large breeds!" Well, as if I need any more evidence... In the case of "should Holden date Claire?" the evidence is solid. Case closed. Gavel slammed. I chuckle, and wink at Holden, who is standing there dumbfounded as I ask, "Claire, are you single?"

"Yes," she responds somewhat hesitantly – maybe she thinks this is a set-up and that my intentions are sinister.

"Well, good. Holden is single, too. Why don't I take your number and I'll have him call you?" Holden is speechless as I pull out my phone and save Claire's number. "Ok, Claire, it was nice meeting you. He'll be in touch!" I say as I motion for Holden to head down the pathway with me toward our cars. "Have a good night!" I wave to Claire.

Halfway to the car, Holden finally finds his voice. "What were you doing back there?"

"What, Holden?" I respond. "We already established that we are better as friends. I can tell that girl is a better fit for you than I am. What's the problem?"

"The problem, Mimi, is that I don't function like that. You were my date for the evening, I didn't want her number," Holden says somewhat angrily.

"Well, why didn't you stop me then?" I ask. Holden is silent. "4-0-7..." I start reading off Claire's number.

"Mimi, I don't want her number!" Holden says with frustration, but I'm still not buying it.

"Whatever, Holden. 4-0-7..." I begin again as he's sitting in his car and pulling his phone out of his pocket. I give him the full number and follow up saying, "I knew you wanted it. Get home safely, Holden" as I walk to my car parked in front of his.

"I'll call you tomorrow, Mimi," he says, breaking my "get-home-safely-tonight" rule once again. I'm hoping he'll call me on my way home, but instead, I get a text at 1:30 a.m.

Holden: I'm puzzled by all of that.

Me: I think you'll thank me later. Ppl try to look over things when there's attraction… I'm trying to see beyond that and think about what matters. I'm very attracted to you physically and I would've liked to explore possibilities, but I know we have deal-breakers that negate us even trying to see where things go.

Holden doesn't call the next day like he said he would. I figure he's back to his old broken promises – leopards don't change their spots. I'm disappointed because, despite our differences, I did want to keep in touch. But it seems that may not happen at this point, until...

Nine days later, out of the blue, I wake up to a text from the previous night at 3:30 a.m.

Holden: I still want that azz Mimi. You have the problems.

turn off #11

Really? How disrespectful! But what should I expect from the man who called his daughter a B? I think because I am so over him, it becomes easy to respond without emotion – at this point, I'm just playing along.

Me: Lol I figured you'd come back. The fact that you're messaging me at 3:30am confirms you want me physically but so does everyone else… I have to filter for those that can be more. Did you call opera girl?

Holden: You are crazy confident. Opera girl asked me to tell her who had the best.

Me: Haaaaaa!! Well if I don't love me, who else will?

Holden: I thought you would like that competition.

Me: Tell her she has the best bc y'all can listen to Soca together while Fido joins you for bedtime.

Holden: You have some balls. I'm going to search for them next time I see you.

Me: Ok Donald Trump 😊

Holden: You are funny!

Me: So, you're not going to tell me if you called her?

Holden: No, I am not going to tell you.

Me: Oh ok.

Holden: I told you. She wants to know who is best? I told her just rubbing up against you was pretty damn impressive.

Me: You got that right ;-) The chemistry was undeniable. I just know what my deal-breakers are… dogs, cigars, religion, as crazy as it sounds. So, could we have some fun nights together? Sure. But for a woman, it needs to be more than physical. So, tell opera girl she wins by default. I dropped out of the race and will give her the prize ;-)

Holden: I can still care about you and have fun nights.

Me: I'm sure you could… and you'd be caring about other women at the same time. I'm not trying to share.

Holden: Your religion is your thing. That's your business. I might have to vouch for your azz at the Pearly Gates so you should pay up in advance. I know other women but I only know one other that would be in your category. However, I do have friends and some of them are friendlier than others, but I don't touch anything I don't like. I don't have a community dick.

Me: Omg your mouth! And from a Christian heading to the pearly gates… Smh. Look, I appreciate that I'm high on your list – at one time you were for me, too, but we just have different ways of handling it.

Holden: We have time. I am just getting out and enjoying a little freedom, but I know quality when I have a 15-minute talk with a person.

Me: I know you do.

Holden: I am still going to be a man with you and try. Remember I don't kiss and tell. What I do is my business and no one else's.

Me: I'd like to see you again but you keep disappearing and I can't trust that you'll honor your commitments… "I'll call tomorrow" then you text a week later…

Holden: I know I have not been good in that regard.

Me: Thank you for owning that.

my crazy #8

Me: Hey, Angie, who you met in Miami, will be in town this weekend for the big bowl game. We're staying on I-drive, you should come by at some point if you have time and we can grab a drink or something.

Holden: I will come and grab something.

Me: Smh…I'm sure those pearly gates are going to lock up as soon as you approach, you are so bad!! I'm the angel!

Before I know it, the weekend has come and gone, and another eight days pass with no word from Holden. I really should let this sleeping dog lie (no pun intended), but I want to invite him out to an upcoming community event despite his transgressions, and I figure I'll bite the bullet. I'm a glutton for punishment.

Me: So much for trying to do better with communication….

Holden (three hours later): I want to get to know you, but you keep telling me to take a hike.

Me: So by me telling you to come and hang out with Angie and me during the bowl game weekend, you interpreted that as me telling you to take a hike?… ok.

Holden: I like your azz. I think you are a quality lady.

Holden (an hour later): No comment?

Me: Wasn't sure how to respond. You know I'm quality, but you talk to me like I'm a piece of meat.

Holden: You are a quality person, but I am the man appreciating you. I did not mean your ass literally. I was referring to the psychological ass if you know what I mean. The one who goes and gets another woman's number for me while I just had a beautiful evening with her.

Me: Ohhhh ok. I almost thought that was what you meant, that I was being an azz for ditching you. [It didn't take long before the name calling began – I guess I should be happy he didn't call me a B *eye roll*] But yes, it was lost in text translation. I can see why you would hold something against me on me passing you off… So how do you wish to proceed now? Don't you have enough women on your hands?

Holden: I only have one other woman here that I talk with. I, unfortunately, don't care for lying so I will always tell you the truth even if it prohibits me from something. You are very interesting to me.

Me: Well that's good to know, I appreciate honesty. And yes, I'm unlike any other woman you'll encounter…

Holden: I believe that.

Me: What are you doing tmw evening?

Holden: I don't have anything at the moment. What's up? Are you planning to spend the night with me?

Me: Of course your mind goes there… No, my friend Giselle is hosting this event tmw evening at 6p on I drive… you think you can join me?

My motivation for letting Holden back in is purely to have him attend this community event and support my friend Giselle, as I'm helping her to promote an event and pack the room.

Holden: Yes. Where and what time?

Me: Awesome, here is the flyer.

Well, Holden shows up for the event the next night, looking dapper as usual, and he is a gentleman the entire night, much like during our prior two outings. We realize during the night that, in addition to my friend Olivia, through whom we initially met and who is in attendance tonight, we have several more mutual friends than we realized. After Holden leaves for the evening, Olivia and our other mutual friends grill me, debating with each other, in front of me, whether or not I should date Holden. "He's too old for her!" "Girl, he's just right!" I could barely get a word in edgewise to tell them my issues with Holden. But after giving them the rundown on the cigars and the hairy dog, they let me off the hook.

Me: Thanks for coming out tonight.

Holden: Was good to see you.

THE VERY UNEXPECTED CONCLUSION

Two weeks pass after the community event, and I haven't heard from Holden. It really doesn't occur to me though – he's out of my mind. It's December, my birthday week, and I'm pulling up a seat to Eddie V's bar with my good friend Tami.

"Girl, what has been going on?" I ask, anxious to catch up with her, as it has been a few months.

"Can I get you ladies something to drink?" the bartender interrupts.

"Yes, we'll each have margarita martinis, the fish tacos, and the calamari – we're celebrating my friend Mimi's birthday," Tami says, motioning towards me. She has always been a good friend. It was her suggestion to treat me to happy hour for my birthday, and the lively bar at Eddie V's with the jazz band playing in the background provides the perfect backdrop for a girls' night out.

Tami turns to me. "Oh, I haven't been up to much, girl, just been working so much, trying to sell houses. I've barely been out," she says.

"Yeah, I bet that takes up a lot of your time," I remark, taking a bite of our calamari appetizer which came out super-quickly.

"So, what about you, girl? What's going on with the men?" Tami asks – everyone knows I'm good for a story.

"Oh, my goodness, girl, it has been so long! So, let me tell you, I met this guy at a fundraiser back in – what? – September? So, three months ago or so," I begin.

Tami interrupts me. "Oh, was he cute? Does he live here?"

I respond excitedly, so ready to tell her the story, "Yes, he has a local investigation practice, and while he's older, *I* consider him attractive."

"So, you know you have to tell me his name," Tami says, wide-eyed like a curious school-kid in the front row of class.

"Oh, his name is Holden Williams – I don't know if you know him..." I say, turning toward her to see her reaction. As soon as I say his name, I already know her answer because it is written all over her face.

She takes a sip of her margarita martini and says, "You know he's married, right?"

I'm puzzled for a moment. "Married?" How could that be? We had talked about that, plus we had several mutual friends. "Hmmm... Are you sure? I'm pretty sure he's separated and going through a divorce," I explain, hoping I have the most up-to-date information.

"You're probably right. I haven't talked to him in some time," Tami explains. *Exhale* I breathe a sigh of relief, though I never really touched the man.

"So, how do you know him?" I ask.

intuition
alarm #7

"Girl, I dated him for 15 years *while* he was married," Tami says. If there was a mic, a speaker, a bullhorn, it would've dropped at that moment. *Say what?!?!* I'm shocked, but at the same time, I shouldn't be too surprised, given that this is my dating life, which means that anything that can go wrong will go wrong. Any information there is to find, I will find it.

Trying not to cast judgment on my friend (though, I have to admit I am looking at her differently), I ask, "Wow, Tami, how did that happen?"

"Well," she explains, "when we met, he told me he was leaving his wife."

I hate to ask, but I know my friend Tami is a magnet for sugar daddies. "Did he buy you things?"

"No, girl, not that much. Just a few little things. But honestly," she goes on, "I really loved him."

Wow. She is spilling green, black, white, and grey tea on me tonight. "Are you ladies doing ok?" the waitress asks. *It depends on your definition of 'ok,'* I think to myself. It's a wonder I haven't fallen out of my bar stool from this news. I'm surprised that my friend was strung along for so many years by this man, shocked that the one guy I tell her about by name this year was her quasi-sugar daddy of yesteryear, and dismayed that the fool lied to me, too, giving me the sob story about his cheating wife, when all the while he was the pumpkin-eater.

"So, did you sleep with him?" Tami asks me, "because you know he has a big one..."

I laugh awkwardly because I'm still uneasy that my friend helped this man commit adultery. While I understand how men can manipulate you and lead you on for years, 15 years is a long time, and I can't help but feel a little perturbed that she took part in that – I don't really want to think about the intimate details of her torrid affair. "I didn't sleep with him; we had too many deal-breakers," I explain as I run them down for her. I tell her that he did turn me on, but that I never even kissed him. And now I'm thanking Jesus, Allah and Buddha that I dodged this lying, cheating, name-calling, 57-year-old bullet. ☺

Take a Page from My Book

I Should've Left this fool in the parking lot the second he called his daughter the B-word – or even prior to that, when he showed he was not a man of his word and broke multiple commitments to call and to meet. There are plenty of lessons learned from ol' 57, including:

- ✓ When you cut a guy off for a good reason, leave him alone. It doesn't get better, even if you feel like fate brought you back together again.

- ✓ If he says he's going to call and he doesn't, don't give him a second, third, or fourth chance to let you down.

- ✓ Be wary of a man who blames his marriage break-up on his cheating spouse and admits no fault of his own.

- ✓ Also, doing a man-cleanse can be good for the mind and soul, leading you to clearer and more successful decision-making... Lady power! ☺

Conclusion

Every man happened to me for a reason. Would I prefer to not get duped by a lying sack of potatoes, or to not waste my time with a man who cheated on his wife for 15 years? Absolutely. But maybe I lived through these experiences for a reason. Maybe it was to have a dynamic story to share. Maybe I can contribute to the national conversation women are having about how *some* men behave, and how we need to be more vocal about calling them out and, when possible, listening to that voice inside that tells us when Mr. Wrong is lurking. No one has all the answers when it comes to choosing a partner in life, but I hope my stories encourage you to use your prior experiences and your intuition as your guide to bringing positive and productive partnerships your way!

About the Author

FAMILY LIFE

Born in the late 70s in Philadelphia, PA to the most loving parents, I describe my upbringing as a very wholesome, happy, all-American childhood. My parents provided a modest home for my older brother and me on their working-class income; we always had what we needed.

Witnessing my parents' almost-50-year marriage over the years has certainly influenced my life decisions. My parents are classic Mars and Venus – mom is an outgoing extrovert who could party and travel all the time, and if she never cooked a meal or washed a dish again in her life, it'd be just fine, while dad is a mellow introvert who could eat home cooking every day, miss virtually every party and every trip, and be just fine. Mom would've preferred more romance, while Dad would've preferred less pomp and circumstance and to just keep it simple. But despite their different ways and desires, they've made it work. Love for their family, respect for each other, and probably a drop of "don't rock the boat" allowed them to stay together. Also, it helps that they're both just really good-hearted people, so there was never a need to part ways. But seeing their dynamics over the years definitely influenced my dating decisions. I acknowledge that I am not as strong as my parents; fundamental compatibility is prime for me – and I do not think my parents are *fundamentally* compatible. It took lots of work and adjustment for them to make it work. Many people of my generation may have left a marriage such as theirs, especially because our generation has a larger pool of dating options than our parents' generation. Plus, most women today have the means to financially support themselves.

In contrast, my mom's mom, born in 1920, also in Philadelphia, was not able to finish high school and, unfortunately, chose a man who turned out to be an alcoholic and who left her to raise three young kids on her own. Until her 50s, my grandmother's options were fairly limited – likely to men she met within a 30-mile radius of her home. Plus, like most women from before my generation, she faced that dire age-25 deadline to meet, marry and mate; if only she knew she was grabbing a not-so-good mate.

But everything happens for a reason. Grandma raised her three children on her own, in the Philadelphia projects, and when she was done, she traveled around the country on church trips, including trips to Hawaii and Canada. She lived until 2007 and in the 30 years I knew her, she never dated. She was probably the happiest, freest person I've ever known. I spent my childhood summers in her 300-square-foot Section 8 efficiency where you could practically eat off the floor because she was so neat and clean. She never even talked about a man, (other than the one good one who died prematurely and unexpectedly in the 1950s). Grandma lived out her golden years in the simplest way – in her words, "doing what I wanna, *when* I wanna," and man-free.

PERSONAL LIFE

So, when I came of age in the 80s and 90s, I was taught that education and a successful career were vital. I watched my mom go to work every day, just like my dad, and there was an unspoken expectation that I would work hard myself one day, after attending college. There was also a societal expectation that I marry and have kids, but I was part of the first generation for which the pressure to do so was not as dire as it had been in the past. Unlike most women before me, I had the freedom to choose to marry, or not, throughout my 30s.

I also had the option of meeting men abroad, so my man-pool was much greater than my mom's or grandmom's. From my first crush, a dirty-blonde-haired blue-eyed boy in my kindergarten class, to the Armenian guy I got horizontal with during a work trip to Germany in my late 20s, to getting chased to my conference hotel room from a Moroccan colleague in Costa Rica, no one can say I haven't had plenty of dating options in my life. Maybe one could argue I've had too many options lol.

Thankfully, I am one of those few women in the world who never dreamed of a wedding day or of having kids (even though I love attracting men and being around kids). Throughout my 20s and 30s, I was constantly told by strangers, friends, and family that I would change my mind, but I have never wavered. I channel my inner Oprah (and Grandma) every day, living my best life, with no pull towards marriage, but if a good Stedman shows up, I would certainly entertain a long-term committed partnership. Heyyy!

The good part about me having zero internal pressures to settle down is that it has allowed me to steer clear of selecting the wrong mate just to beat my biological clock. My clock was clearly broken anyway, and thank goodness because if I had to choose from the men who have crossed my path, I imagine I'd be divorced – or in jail – by 40 lol.

Ah, but alas, today, I am incredibly happy and single at 40 years of age. My family and friends are my soul mates, and I'm proud to say with confidence that I can live a full and fulfilled life just as I am today. #bestlife #fulllife #canbehappilysingle #iknowme #loveme

PROFESSIONAL LIFE

I am an auditor by nature. I question everything and allow logic to guide my decisions. I have worked for what was the largest accounting firm in the world. When it sank in 2002, I began writing stories on my dating life to entertain my co-workers who suddenly had no work to do – leading to this book. Later in my career, I shifted to compliance and risk management for one of Orlando's largest theme parks, and later for a large telecom provider. But always thinking about "what could go wrong" for a business flowed over into my personal life; I constantly analyze relationships, waiting for the shoe to drop, and mildly trusting, but always verifying. Great trait at work, maybe not as good for the personal life, but just can't turn it off!

I have a Bachelor's in Accounting, an MBA, an international audit certification, and I serve on several professional and charitable boards. I am Mimi Mansfield .

71172794R00136

Made in the USA
Columbia, SC
26 August 2019